"Not many people can laugh their way through cancer. But Chuck Walton did. He even wrote a book about it. The book takes the reader on a surprisingly funny foray into the world of stage four metastatic melanoma."

Kathe Brunton,
Feature writer, Goshen Health Systems Annual Report

"This is a fascinating story about a cancer survivor who helps all of us come to grips with what really matters in life. It is quick reading, funny and inspiring."

Doug Schwartzentruber, MD, FACS
Medical Director, Center for Cancer Care

"Standing Up To Cancer: Mishawaka (Indiana) man maintains positive outlook and shares it with others."

Kim Kilbride, South Bend Tribune

"Love this book, very inspiring and a joy to read!"

Linda Buell, Signs Etc.

"Great Book!"

Emily Bartos, ND, LAc, Center for Cancer Care

"Laughter renews, revives, and relieves; and this book is hugely renewing, reviving, and relieving. From the very first paragraph, Chuck engages and inspires the rest of us with his ability to laugh in the face of cancer, mammoth flies, and angry clocks. Thanks for a great book that I can pass along to others!"

Rita Gingrich, MSW, PNI Counselor
Center for Cancer Care

"In spirit, we will always be."

Charles Walton

ALMOST ALWAYS FATAL

(Surviving Cancer with a Sense of Humor)

by

Charles Walton

Published by: KC CREATIONS, Inc.
1040 Bancroft circle, Suite C
Mishawaka, IN 46544-3630

ISBN: 978-0-6151-5361-2

You can write to the author at: <u>charleswalton1@yahoo.com</u>

This is for my wife Kathy - my soul-mate.

And my children:
Andy
Sean
Autumn
Rebecca
Ryan
And their families.

I love you all.

"Love and laughter come from the soul,

and *feed* the soul.

There is no greater healing power anywhere."

Charles Walton

ACKNOWLEDGEMENTS

There's no real way to show my appreciation to all the people from the medical community who helped me through this ordeal. Every one of you played an important role in my story, and many of you I credit directly with helping to save my life. You will all forever hold a special place in my heart.

From The Center for Cancer Care in Goshen, Indiana:

Douglas Schwartzentruber, MD, FACS Medical Director, Surgical Oncologist - Goshen Center for Cancer Care

Debbie Snyder, RN, BSN, OCN – Clinic Nurse

Kristan Rheinheimer, RN, MSN, FNP, OCN, Nurse Practitioner

Deana Gonyon, RN, MSN, ANP, ARNP-BC, Nurse Practitioner

Emily Bartos , ND, LAc

Sara Swartzentruber – Scheduler

Pat Vandenburg, RN – Care Coordinator

Linda Butler – Scheduler

David Penrose, MA

Rita Gingrich, MSW, PNI Counselor

Melissa Rone – Public Relations Coordinator

Linda Bontrager, RN

Janell Bontrager, RN

Sue Dolby, RN

Twilight Douma, RN

Kathy Freed, RN

Carol Fuller, RN

Alice Hershberger, RN

Marlene Hershberger, RN

Beth Jones, RN

Patti Kauffman, NA

Linda Kurtz, NA

Brooke Martin, RN

Lynne Medlock, RN

Rhoda Miller, RN

Marcia Powell, RN

Betsy Schrock, RN

Deborah Shetler, RN

Sharon Swihart, RN

Micah Thieszen, RN

Pacu Staff

Bonnie Blosser, RN

Cindy Daily, RN

Jo Lovette, RN

Dina Patti, RN

Anna Wong, RN

Sam Zheng, MD

From Phelps' Office of Dermatology, South Bend, Indiana:

Stephen R. Phelps, MD

From Memorial Lymphedema Program, South Bend, Indiana

Roger G. Klauer, MD

Amy Kuitse, OTR, CLT-LANA

Jane Philips, RN, MS, OCN

A POINT OF FACT

In order for this work to have been considered "book length", it had to meet certain criteria concerning number of words, number of pages, etc. I feel it my humble duty to point out that I may not have been able to "make the grade" if Dr. Schwartzentruber's surname had been Sims, or Kent, or Tate. I think you see what I mean.

A SPECIAL THANKS

Dr. Schwartzentruber, my friend, I'll never be able to express adequately the confidence you instilled in me throughout this whole ugly mess with your professionalism, genuine knowledge, and honest-to-God good and caring heart. I believe you are, as they say, an "old soul" because you have wisdom beyond your years. Thank you.

Cancer Survivor: "I once heard it said that you should be considered a survivor from the moment you're diagnosed with the cancer."

Douglas Schwartzentruber, MD, FACS

FOREWORD

(Don't skip the Foreword)

I often skip the "Foreword" myself, but then I invariably find myself reading it *after*ward because I'm afraid I might have missed something. In this case, you will have missed my explanation of why I'm writing this book in the first place. Of course I'm not actually writing it in the *first* place. That would seem to imply that I have never done anything else, which I assure you I have. I am writing it in the first *person* however, if that's any consolation.

As you shall soon see, when I found out that I had a life-threatening cancer I wondered, "Why me?" as I'm sure many do in similar circumstances. Now that I'm coming out the other side, I again find myself wondering, "Why me?" I know, personally, two different people who died from the very same cancer. Why them and not me? I'm not, after all, any more special than they were, or than you are, in any way. The conclusion I've come to is that I am supposed to share my experience with you so that you might take away from it something that benefits you in your life's challenges, especially if you are in a place where you think things couldn't get much worse. Not only do I believe that I *must* do this, I also believe that, in the telling of my story to you, I am supposed to call upon my own sense of humor to help me to reach you, because, dear reader, if while ingesting these words, a smile forms upon your face, or a chuckle escapes you involuntarily, you will already have begun to realize one of the most powerful internal medicines we, as spiritual beings having a human experience, have in our arsenal against sickness and despair. Laughter is such a positive force.

If there is any one thing in particular that I hope you take away from this reading, it's the realization that positive influences are what cause you to thrive, and negative influences only drag you down and do their damnedest to keep you down. Positive energy is just that, it's good because its source is goodness. Negative energy comes from darkness and can only hurt you.

I looked on the internet for information concerning my specific cancer and I found one support group where I saw the words, "is almost always fatal" over and over again. Some support! I had a couple of doctors who also seemed to think it a catchy little phrase. You'll see that the farther I put myself from these kinds of influences, and the closer to the positive, the better off I was - although I suppose I should be grateful for having been supplied with the perfect title for my book. No, I take that back. Don't ever be beholding in any way to anyone who brings you the negative, but love those people with all your heart who bring you hope. I intend to be one of them.

FINDING OUT

So, I have cancer. Great. So now what?

I wish I could say I was that blasé about it when I first heard the news. And outwardly, I must admit, to my friends and family I probably appeared to handle it well. But the fact is, on the inside, I was more like this: Oh God! Why me? What have I done to deserve this? Oh poor, poor me! Why? Why? I knew I should have gone to church, or been nicer to people, or both. Ok, I'll start now. No, it's too late. Damn! No, not damn, darn. This is no time to cuss for Christ's sake! What did I just *say*? Cussing is probably what got me here in the first place. I'm a cusser; face it. And what kind of people cuss? The kind who deserve to get cancer, that's what kind!

That's right, I'm being punished. That has to be it. And I deserve it too, don't I? Of course I do. I could have been a better person in my fifty-two years. I didn't have to be so cynical of other people and their disgusting habits did I? Did I have to, even mentally, make fun of the fat man hurrying across a restaurant parking lot to get his food fix while I smugly enjoyed a cigarette in the comfort of my car? No, I didn't. And what *about* those cigarettes, cancer sticks, coffin nails?

Haven't I been smoking for over thirty-five years just *daring* cancer to pay me a visit? Well sure, *lung* cancer maybe, but stage-three melanoma ("which is almost always fatal")? How is *that* fair? And shouldn't life always be fair to me? Aren't I special? Isn't this something that happens to someone else, not me?

Like I said, on the inside things were not what they appeared to be from without. But, do you know what? Over two years have now passed since the initial "finding out" and I'm not dead. Ok. You knew that. Can't slip anything past *you*, eh? But it appears that the stage-three melanoma ("which is almost always fatal") is backing off, even reversing itself. How can this be, you ask? Was it some new medical technology? Were you introduced to a spiritual healer? Did you find a way to tap the power of your own soul to heal your body? Were you the recipient of many heartfelt prayers? Did someone give you a magical elixir from ancient Asia? In answer to the above questions I would have to say yes, or at least I believe so, to all of them.

In order for you to fully understand what I just said, I think I'm going to have to tell you the whole story. Not *my* whole story. Good grief. That would cover fifty-two years! Nope, this story just covers my struggle with metastatic melanoma - stage three - ("which is almost always fatal") and how, in just over the last two years or so, I've gone from the chaos, inner turmoil, and fear of discovering I had a life threatening disease, to having found a new peacefulness, and contentedness that has helped to put me well on my way to not only a cancer-free life, but a life of a much better quality than I've ever known before.

THE SPOTTING OF THE SPOT

It's 1986, early autumn. I'm living in South Bend, Indiana and driving a gasoline tanker for a company in Niles, Michigan (about four miles from my house). I'm at home this day and I notice a light brown spot on my left inner calf about the size of a dime and approximately the shape of Florida. It's new. I've never laid eyes on it before.

Every two years I'm required, as a commercial driver's license

holder, to get a new D.O.T (Department of Transportation) physical.
The time for the physical rolls around; I go.

I say, "Hey Doc, What d'ya think about this thing on my leg?"

He says, "It looks kind of like Florida doesn't it?"

"Yeah." I say. "But do you think it's anything I should be
concerned about? It's new."

"Nah, it doesn't look like anything much to me. Turn your head
and cough for me, will ya?"

I didn't think a whole lot more about it and I went on with my
life just as if I knew what I was doing. It's not like there was nothing
else going on in my life for me to think about either. I was divorced
that year and that was the year I tried to get out of truck driving by
buying a deli on the south side of South Bend. That was great for a
while, mainly because my kids could come and hang out with me there.
They liked helping out. We had Easter dinner there that year for the
whole family. It was great being my own boss and feeling like I had
some control over my own future. Apparently it wasn't meant to be at
that particular time though because the business didn't make it. It

turned out the previous owners had padded their books with rental income from their twenty-something rental properties. Surprise! I did everything within my power to make that business work. I got my old job back driving a gasoline tanker and used my paycheck to pay my employees. We tried starting up pizza delivery and my sister, Brenda, even came in and managed the deli for me for free, just to help out.

That was also the year I was stabbed twice in my right side . . . What? Ok, I'll tell you about that, briefly.

I had just picked up a load of ethanol from the big plant on the west side of South Bend and I was driving down the on-ramp to the northbound U.S. 31 bypass when I saw an old beat-up green van on the shoulder of the road, out of gas. I figured it was out of gas mainly because there was a guy standing near the right-hand rear corner of it holding up a red gas can and waving it frantically in my direction. I hadn't picked up much speed yet so I pulled my truck over in front of the van, got out, and walked around the front to the non-traffic side where the guy met me halfway down the length of my rig. He was a nasty-looking son of a gun up close.

He was wearing a dingy, stained T-shirt that had probably been white at some time in the long-distant past. His hair was a greasy brown and his eyes, as they met mine, were crazy-green, and I *do* mean crazy. He looked like he was high on something.

The guy spit tobacco juice on the ground and produced a lock-blade knife with about a six-inch blade at the same time. Then he screamed at me.

"Gimme yer money!" He dropped the gas can he'd been carrying on the ground by his left foot. At this same moment, another guy appeared from between the front of the old van and the rear of my tanker trailer. He was bigger than Crazy-Eyes with black hair and the same disheveled, dirty appearance. He looked down the highway behind us and then stayed put, watching. What had I gotten myself into?

I knew that I had only fifteen dollars in my wallet so I reached for it. It was in my right-hand back pocket. I would just give it to them and get out of there. I wasn't armed and this didn't feel like one of my foolish days (which I've had from time to time).

"I've only got about fifteen bucks." I said, opening my wallet in front of me. I was watching Crazy-Eyes closely. I saw his eyes drop to my left wrist as I started to take the bills from my wallet.

My brother had given me a nice gold watch, which he had purchased for me when stationed in Saudi Arabia as a Marine M.P. security guard at the United States embassy there. It meant a lot to me at the time.

"Gimme that watch too, and that ring!" He took a step forward. Black-Hair looked nervously around again, but stayed where he was.

The ring Crazy-Eyes wanted was about the only thing I had left of my dad, who had died when I was only six years old. It was just a gold band, his wedding ring from his marriage to my mother. I wore it on my "pinky" finger on my right hand.

"I'll give you the fifteen bucks." I said. "But you're not getting the ring or the watch." Crazy-Eyes looked furious.

"Take 'em off!" He screamed. I shoved the bills back into my wallet and slid it into the back pocket of my jeans (Ok, so maybe it *was* one of those days).

With no more warning, this sleaze-ball lunged forward. I stumbled backward. He jammed the knife into the right side of my body, to the hilt. I felt my skin rip open and give way to the cold steel blade, and then the mind-numbing burn as he yanked the knife back out.

Black-Hair came running toward us yelling at Crazy-Eyes.

"Just take the money, man! Just take the money and let's get outa here!" I started backing up, watching them both. I didn't know if Black-Hair was going to decide to jump on me or what. I was holding my right hand against the place where I had been stabbed. Although I didn't dare take my eyes off the two creeps in front of me, I could feel the warmth of my own blood oozing through my fingers; they were slippery with it.

The man with the insanely furious green eyes jabbed the knife at me again and I grabbed for his arm. My hand was too slick with blood to make purchase but I did manage to avoid the blade that time. Black-Hair had now reached Crazy-Eyes and was attempting to pull him backward, shouting that they had to get out of there. I stopped and just stood looking at the two of them. I couldn't turn my back on them and I was acutely aware of how badly I was bleeding. I couldn't seem to come up with anything that even remotely resembled an offensive plan of action. It seemed surreal, like a dream, except for the burning.

Suddenly Crazy-Eyes screamed something unintelligible and jerked himself free of Black-Hair's grip and ran straight for me. I tried to sidestep and knock him aside as I had done before, but this time the blade made it to its mark and he stabbed me very near the first wound. The difference this time was that when he tried to yank the knife back out of my flesh, it was so slick with blood that his hand slipped off of it.

I now had possession of the weapon! Of course I didn't feel very menacing with it imbedded in my side.

Black-Hair had Crazy-Eyes by the T-shirt now and was forcing him back, still yelling that they had to get out of there, that a cop was going to come along. Those rabid-green, dilated eyes looked directly into mine as he backed away, no longer resisting. Just briefly, for an instant, I saw confusion, as if he were trying to figure out what had just happened.

I walked backward, toward the cab of my truck. I still wouldn't turn my back on them, and I was hurting. They both climbed into their van. I heard the clatter of their engine as they sped away. I couldn't see them. I was still on the shoulder side of my truck. I made my way around to the traffic side and looked for them, thinking maybe I could remember their plate number, but they were long gone. I remembered that they had had a Texas plate on the van but I hadn't had any reason to make note of the number when I had first pulled over to help.

I was hoping a police officer would come along while there was still time to chase them down, but that didn't happen and I still had the bleeding thing going on. I decided that I'd better get myself somewhere where I could get some help. I climbed into the cab of my truck and took off north on the highway toward Michigan. Every time I shifted gears or hit a bump in the road, the blade of that knife would jostle around inside me and cause me to gasp in pain. It's even possible that I might have used a few choice cuss words. In fact, I'm guilty of that for sure. The burning was excruciating though. I was bleeding so much from the first wound, and from around the blade of the knife, that I was afraid to pull it out. It was pretty obvious that if I began to leak from the second wound as much as I was from the first, I would, very soon, be a much less colorful character in my own story.

In my now somewhat fuzzy mind, I thought that if I could just get to my company's truck terminal, they would help me. The problem was, after driving about six miles, I realized I was too light-headed to continue so I pulled the truck off onto the shoulder of the highway. I remember looking down at the floor of my truck and seeing what appeared to be a big puddle of red paint all around the bottom of the shifter and running under the seat. I was momentarily irritated by this gross negligence and dumbfounded that anyone could just walk away and *leave* a mess like that. Then, of course, I realized that "mess" had come from me, and I climbed down from the cab. I was careful not to bump the handle of the knife, very careful, believe me.

I was kind of half bent over, holding my side and trying to keep the blade still, when an old green van pulled up behind my truck. Old green van? Are you thinking what I was thinking? I was seeing through a fog by this time from the loss of blood and the first thing that came into my mind was that the two sleaze-bags had come back to finish me off. Those bastards! (There I go again with the cussing!) It turned out to be a very nice elderly gentleman though, and he gave me a ride to my terminal. He tried to get me to let him take me directly to the hospital but, in my state of mind, I thought it was more important that my company know where their truckload of ethanol was parked. Ethanol is a hazardous substance after all. I still don't think I did the wrong thing in that regard.

I got out of the nice man's van after we pulled in to the terminal parking lot and promptly passed out. I woke up in an ambulance, heading for the hospital, sirens blaring, and discovered I had apparently made the correct decision about the knife. The paramedics wouldn't pull it out either, for the same reason. A doctor would do that later, after x-rays and such. I conked back out.

When next I awoke I was disoriented. I didn't know where I was. My eyes were still closed and my side was burning, but there was an even more terrible burning in my nose and throat. Something was in there! It was a worm! No, a stick. I grabbed it and began pulling it out. I opened my eyes and tried to see what it was, almost afraid to look. It was some kind of plastic tube. Who would *do* such a thing! I had it almost all the way out now. Good God, how it burned! There. It was out. Whew! I surveyed the room I was in, a hospital room. A hospital room? Then it all came back to me and I gazed down at the messy, clear-plastic tube on the bed where I had dropped it. *I'll bet I wasn't supposed to take that out.* I thought. Then in came a nurse. She had a kind of no-nonsense way of walking. I tried to hide the tube under the sheet before she had a chance to see it.

"Well, you're awake Mr. Wal.... What did you do!" Geez, she was good.

"It was burning my nose and my throat." I explained.

"You shouldn't have done that." She said sternly. "I don't believe you did that!"

"Well, I didn't know what it was." I protested weakly.

"So what'd you think?" She demanded. That somebody put a stick or something up your nose for no good reason?" She held up the tube menacingly. "This is the tube from your stomach pump. It has to be monitored to see what comes up. Now I'm going to have to insert it all over again." She exhaled a sigh of resignation and then suddenly smiled and patted my hand. "You know," she said, now with a malicious twinkle in her eye, "the first time I inserted this thing, you were asleep . . ."

It turned out there was no permanent damage (from the knife I mean), no vital organs punctured, and after a few days in the hospital I went home.

Oh yes, I did find out from the police report the name of the elderly gentleman who had stopped to help me. I called him to say thank you and to find out if I could pay to have his van professionally cleaned. I knew I had to have bled all over his passenger seat. He wouldn't hear of it. He said all it took was some soap and water, and a little "elbow grease". I asked him if I could take him, and his wife, out for dinner. He wouldn't accept that either. He said anybody would have done what he did if they had seen me all crouched over, soaked in blood on the side of the road like that. I hope that's true, but I'm not so sure.

I finally got him to agree to allow me to send him a gift certificate for "dinner for two" at his wife's favorite restaurant. That way he could tell himself he was doing it for her and not feel as though he were accepting payment for a good deed. He had his pride you see. I understood that. He was a good man and I knew, when I heard he had passed on a few years ago, that he was going to a good place.

They never caught the bad guys, by the way.

My point in telling you that story is to express how there were other things happening in my life which demanded more immediate attention than the dime-sized replica of Florida on the calf of my left leg.

At the next D.O.T physical, two years later, I was in a different place, with a different doctor, and when I pointed out the spot on my leg, he reacted pretty much the same way as had the doctor two years prior. Once again, I thought there was no cause for concern.

KATHY

In the spring of 1989 my wife Kathy came in to my life to stay. I say, "to stay" because we had originally met eleven years earlier at my sister's wedding. All these years later she came down from her home in Waterloo, Ontario, Canada to visit with my sister, Brenda. I dropped over to Brenda's house to say hello. I was still single and, lo and behold, it turned out Kathy had been divorced about a year. We both realized right away that there was something special between us that may have actually been there since the first time we'd met. Of course it had never been acknowledged because eleven years prior we had both been attached to other people.

When Kathy returned to Canada after that visit, we spoke on the telephone so often that her phone bills were running somewhere in the vicinity of the stratosphere and mine were double that!

Kathy and her three children moved to Indiana and we were married on December 30, 1989. Sixteen years later, all five of our kids are grown, two with families of their own, and we are more happily married than ever. She is my foundation; she is the glue that has held me together through all of this cancer business.

Way back in 1989 Kathy asked, "What's that thing on your leg, a birthmark?"

"It just showed up in '86." I said. "Why? Do you think it looks like something?"

"Yeah." She said. "It looks a lot like Florida and I think you should have it checked out." I told her that the doctors I'd already shown it to didn't seem to think it was any big deal.

"Besides," I pointed out. "Look at old Gorbachev. He's had Florida or Guatemala, or some such nonsense right there on top of his *head* for all the world to see for a long, long time. If there was anything to *that* I'm sure some doctor, somewhere, would have said something about it by now. This thing of mine is probably like that."

Of course Kathy, caring wife that she is, wasn't happy with that answer. The next time I came down with a bad cold or flu and needed an antibiotic, she made an appointment for me to see *her* doctor and reminded me to have her take a look at my leg. Kathy had only been in the states a short time and already had found a doctor while I, after living here my whole life, didn't really have anyone I saw regularly.

Kathy's doctor asked me if the spot had changed. I told her that, aside from the fact that it didn't used to be there at all, it was pretty much the same. Her assessment then, was the same as the previous doctors'. She said it didn't really look like any big deal.

You may have noticed that I haven't used any of these doctors' names. At first I was more than just a little bit bitter about their cavalier attitudes concerning my leg. You see, if I had caught the cancer back then it never would have got to be *stage three* melanoma ("which is almost always fatal"). It could have been removed and that probably would have been the end of it. But then, it was (and still is) *my* leg. I should have taken it more seriously myself. I just had this crazy idea that if I asked the doctors and *they* didn't think I needed to be concerned and have it checked out further, I could relax about it, put it out of my mind. Silly me, huh?

FLORIDA RISES

Fifteen years sailed by and the year became 2004. The years

really did seem to sail too. One day the kids were just that, and the next they are all adults and we have *grandkids* for crying out Pete's sake!

In September of 2004 Kathy and I were running our two-year-old business from our home. It was a small trucking company. We had three tractors, three trailers, and three drivers. We were struggling, but we were working together and that made it worthwhile.

In, I think, June of that year one of the trucks broke down in Charlotte, North Carolina. The driver said the transmission had gone out. Of the ten gears he should have had available, he had only sixth gear. I called the national road service we used and they recommended a repair shop in Charlotte (which I shall also not name). I instructed the driver to baby the truck over there. The shop owner informed me over the telephone that all the transmission oil had leaked out and that the "tranny" was now junk.

That truck was down for about three weeks and cost us a bucket-load of dough to fix. We also paid for the driver's transportation to and from home where he sat on salary while the truck was in the shop because we didn't want to lose him. It wasn't *his* fault he couldn't work. On a big truck, the driver can't check the level of the transmission oil, in case you were thinking that he should have. It's not accessible like it is on a car. Of course the revenue from that truck was zilch at the same time all that money was going out.

The next month, in July, one of our other drivers pulled out into the path of another big truck on the highway. Thank God neither driver was hurt, but the front-end of our truck was ripped off and smashed to smithereens.

I had heard stories throughout my life of various things being "smashed to smithereens", but I had never actually *seen* a smithereen. Now I have. It is not something easily forgotten. As a matter of fact, if you were to come to my house today, you would see, sitting on my desk as a constant reminder to "look both ways", a single unwashed smithereen.

So now we have another truck down, this time for two months. Insurance is paying for this repair but they are *not* paying the monthly payment on the truck or the ongoing insurance premiums and, of course, this truck is bringing in no revenue either.

Somewhere around the time the wrecked truck was again roadworthy, and I had hired a new driver for it, two things happened: First, the truck that had just had the transmission repaired in North Carolina broke down again in Michigan with the exact same problem. It seems that the yahoos at the repair shop put in a "new rebuilt" transmission but they didn't replace the transcooler which was the part that was leaking the oil in the first place. Obviously, now the second transmission was ruined too. The repair shop refused to make good on, what I considered to be, their negligence. I would have had to hire an attorney in North Carolina to pursue the matter and the mechanic in Michigan said he wasn't going to get involved in any litigation. He wouldn't make any kind of sworn statement or testify in court. So that truck was down again, making no money, and we had to eat the cost.

The other thing that occurred, around this same time, was that I noticed that the dime-sized thing on my left leg had changed. Florida had risen substantially. It had also spread out so that now it was about the size of a nickel and more closely resembled Texas than it did

Florida.

I didn't have time for this nonsense but at Kathy's insistence - she seemed to care more about me than I did - my leg and I went to see an actual dermatologist: Dr. Stephen Phelps in South Bend.

I asked Dr. Phelps if he would remove this nasty-looking thing from my leg. I explained to him how it used to look like Florida, and how it was now Texas with a mountain range and besides, it was just plain ugly. He took one look at it and promptly informed me, in no uncertain terms, that he would definitely *not* be removing it. He said he didn't like the looks of it one bit and that what he *would* do, would be to take a deep sample of it and send it off to the lab.

The next day Dr. Phelps called and said the lab had confirmed his initial concern: The alien thing on my leg was melanoma and it was in what appeared to be an advanced stage. He said we needed to deal with this right away. He set up appointments for me to see both a plastic surgeon and a vascular surgeon the following day. Dr. Phelps made these appointments and started the ball rolling on this thing personally. I mean he made the calls to the other doctors, and to me, *himself.* That may not seem like such a big deal, but believe me in this day and age it is. It mattered to me. It caused me to realize the seriousness of the situation immediately.

Like I said earlier, there are doctors who are part of my story but whom I shall not name because I believe my continued association with them would have been extremely detrimental to my well-being. The doctors and others I *do* name however, are the persons I believe are directly responsible for the fact that I haven't yet come down with a serious case of death. Dr. Phelps is the first of these very excellent, professional, caring, and conscientious human beings.

No more than a week after seeing Dr. Phelps that first time, I had undergone two separate surgeries, - which I will tell you about in a minute - several tests and procedures, and I had racked up over $50,000 in medical bills. I didn't know it at the time, but that was just the beginning.

I brought up the money for a reason: I had no health insurance. Being self-employed, I had put off getting health insurance because it was so expensive. If memory serves me, it was over seven hundred dollars per month for Kathy, our youngest son Ryan, and me. I just didn't think I could squeeze that amount in to the already-tight budget on which we were operating. Obviously, in hindsight, I can see that I should have found a way to cram it in there. We were all healthy you see. I mean, what could happen?

TEXAS - A LONE STAR?

Back to the surgery: The doctors told me they needed to remove the *tumor*, which was a word I had shied away from, just like the "C" word. After the plastic surgeon removed the tumor and did a skin graft over the area with a little section he would take from my thigh, the vascular surgeon would then remove the sentinel lymph nodes - the ones closest to the tumor. They wanted to find out if the cancer had metastasized - traveled.

The lymph nodes are found through a procedure known as nuclear medicine. A different doctor shot a radioactive substance into my leg very near the "Texas" border, and this substance made its way to all the lymph nodes in my left leg. I guess they then glowed in the dark or something because they had no trouble finding and marking them with a Sharpie so the surgeons would be able to find them later.

The doctor who administered the nuclear medicine technology told me it would be very, *very* painful and it was, but it sure beat the heck out of having them open up my leg and just go prowling around in there on a lymph node finding expedition.

When I woke up in the hospital room Kathy was, of course, sitting there waiting for me to come around. She smiled at my silly, groggy face and I was once again reminded of just how very important she is to me. She is always there for me. I could see the concern and the love in her eyes as she welcomed me back into the conscious world.

"It's about time." She said, as she kissed me on the cheek. "You were really gone there, you know?"

"You mean they're finished?" I asked, taking in my surroundings and shaking off the feeling of disorientation.

"Yes." she said. "Look how big the bandage on your leg is." She folded the sheet and blanket back over my leg so I could see it.

Thick bandages covered pretty much all of my leg between my

foot and my knee.

"That *does* seem like a lot." I said. "Considering the tumor was only about the size of a nickel. Hey. What's this?" I had found another bandage on my thigh where the sentinel lymph nodes had been removed.

"Lymph nodes." confirmed Kathy. "Five of them."

"Oh, yeah." I said. "So, what did they find?"

"I don't know." She said. "Nobody has told me anything. I don't think the results are back from the lab yet." Kathy gently laid her hand on the bandage covering my calf. I thought I saw the flicker of a frown cross her face.

"What's the matter?" I asked.

"What? Oh, nothing. I just thought your bandage looked like it was wrapped kind of . . . funny. I think it was just the way it was reflecting the light. You know, a shadow or something."

After Kathy left late that afternoon, having been at the hospital with me since 7:30 that morning, I found another big rectangular bandage on my outer thigh. *What's this?* I wondered as I drifted off to sleep. *Must be a spare.*

The next morning, shortly after Kathy arrived, the vascular surgeon came in to see me.

"Hello, Mr. Walton. You're looking rested."

"I am." I said. "So what's the scoop on the ol' nodes, Doc?" He glanced at Kathy then back at me.

"Well, the surgery went just fine." He said. "Very smooth. No problems at all. But the lab results show that the first four of the five lymph nodes I removed *did* have microscopic bits of melanoma."

So the "lone star" wasn't so alone after all. That was *not* what I had expected to hear.

Kathy stood, walked over and took my hand in hers.

"I hate it when that happens." I joked halfheartedly. I didn't think it was funny though. I knew what it meant. It had all been explained to Kathy and me before the surgery.

"I would like to remove the rest of the lymph nodes in that leg right away." Said the doctor. "But first we need to schedule you for a PET/CT scan to see if the cancer shows up anywhere else in your body."

"And if it does?" That was I.

"Well, if we see that it's already in other parts of your body there would be no point in taking out the rest of the lymph nodes and causing you to have to deal with lymphedema on top of everything else."

I said, "There would be no point in taking out the rest of the lymph nodes because it would be too late?" Kathy was squeezing my hand tightly as we both waited for the surgeon's answer, even though we both already knew what it was.

"Mr. Walton, Mrs. Walton," His face told the story. "We now know that the melanoma has metastasized. We know that it is *stage three* melanoma. We also know that metastatic melanoma is very often ("almost always") fatal. But let's not be too pessimistic at this point (Yeah, let's not). Let me get that scan ordered and we'll go from there."

"Ok." I said. What else *could* I say? *Let's just forget about this whole thing doc. I'll just get up and go home now and we'll pretend this never happened. Just ignore it right? And it will go away.*

I tried that once though. I already knew it wouldn't work. Ignoring it just made things worse.

Kathy and I held on to each other after the doctor left. We didn't say much. We just held on.

THE SHARK BITE

Forty-eight hours after that first surgery, the plastic surgeon came in to change my bandage. Kathy was on her way up but she hadn't yet arrived.

As the doctor and I shook hands he said, "Now, when I unwrap this leg, I may think that it looks perfectly fine, as I'm sure it will. You, on the other hand, may not necessarily agree with me about that. You must remember, I have seen many of these, but this is your first."

"And it's *my* leg." I said.

"And it's *your* leg. That's true." He began to carefully remove the bandage.

The doctor had pulled the curtain the length of the bed for

privacy so I didn't see Kathy when she came in the room. She came to the end of the curtain at the foot of my bed just as the doctor gently pulled free the final layer of gauze. Her movement caught my eye and I just barely got a glimpse of her face. Her eyes moved down to my leg at the precise moment the gauze was peeled away. There was a millisecond of horror on her face and she was gone. When she saw what the doctor had uncovered she had immediately turned around and left the room. She didn't know I had seen her and she didn't want me to see her initial reaction to the raw wound on my leg.

Realizing she was there, seeing her shocked expression, and then looking down at the wound myself, took less than a second I'm sure, but it seemed as though it were taking place in slow motion. And then I couldn't tear my eyes away from my leg. Remember, "Texas" was only nickel-size. This red, wet-looking nastiness on my leg looked as though a small shark had just bitten a huge chunk out of my calf.

"You're right." I said to the doc. "I *don't* like the way it looks."

"A normal reaction." He said. "That's why I warned you."

"Well," I said. "You need to beef up your warning just a tad if you ask me. That's a big chunk of meat missing there!"

He said, "Yes, it seems that way to you, but we had to be sure and remove all the surrounding tissue that might be affected by the melanoma. I wanted to make certain we got it all. I think it looks very good. It's coming along nicely. You've probably noticed a large rectangular bandage on your thigh." (The spare.) "That's where we removed the thin layer of tissue with which we grafted the wound."

"So that's what all the stitches around the edges of the shark-bite are for." I said. "To hold that thin layer in place. It must be *very* thin. It looks like it's just raw muscle." I still couldn't believe such a big hunk of my calf was gone. It was almost a perfect oval shape and the skin graft was literally so thin you could see right through it. My muscle tissue was very red and the whole thing appeared moist and spongy. There were sutures all around the rim of the oval that reminded me of the stitching on a baseball. No wonder Kathy had taken one look and disappeared! She returned about this time and kissed me on the cheek.

The doctor nodded a hello to her and then responded.

"Shark-bite?" he said, looking puzzled. "At any rate, I can assure you there *is* a graft there, but you're correct, it is very thin so it looks a little raw now. Soon enough it will be more pink than red."

Kathy's eyes met mine and she asked the question.

"So it's always going to look like there's a big piece missing?"

"Well, Yes." the doctor said. "There *is* a big piece missing. It's not going to grow back. That's the whole reason for the graft. You can't sew closed a wound of that size."

I was instructed on the care of my wounds and had my PET/CT scan before leaving the hospital that day. Kathy took me home where we resumed the helm of the sinking ship we called our business while awaiting the results.

The vascular surgeon's office called the following day and said the scans had produced negative results, which was positive news. That same telephone conversation also produced a new surgery date, which I asked them to move back one more week so I could vote in the upcoming elections (I know, I know, but I *always* vote if possible).

The doctor wanted to get the rest of the lymph nodes out of that leg as soon as possible. There was no discussion of any possible alternative therapy.

THE JAGGED EDGE

Once again I found myself waking up in a hospital room with Kathy in a chair at my bedside reading a book. We just had time to say hello and smooch before the doctor walked in.

"Well Mr. Walton, it seems we have some good news this time. The rest of the lymph nodes in the effected leg, all fifteen of them, were clean. No sign of melanoma." Kathy squeezed my hand. Her eyes were glistening as she asked,

"Does this mean that it's over? That you got it all? It's all gone?"

"We hope so." Said the doctor. "We know these lymph nodes were clean, we know the blood work and the scan results were negative, but you must remember that in order for anything to show up on the scan, it has to be about the size of half your little fingernail. The microscopic amounts we found in the first four of the five sentinel

nodes wouldn't have shown up in a scan."

"But if *all fifteen* of the lymph nodes were clean . . ." I began.

"Oh this is definitely a good sign." He said. "Don't get me

wrong. We'll just have to keep an eye on things now. As matter of

fact, I'm going to refer you to an oncologist to follow up. My staff will

call you with an appointment. He will be the one who will monitor

your progress, not me. I've done all I can at this point. The oncologist

will, no doubt, want to do periodic scans and blood work. I'll also refer

you to another doctor for treatment of the lymphedema you will be

developing now that you have no lymph nodes in this leg." He patted

my leg. He then proceeded to remove the bandage from my brand new

wound.

As he did this, I couldn't help but notice there was a clear plastic

tube sticking out of a hole in my thigh about the diameter of a pencil

(and no, I didn't try to pull it out). It was on the top of my thigh

approximately half way between my groin and my knee.

"Hey Doc, I think you forgot something here. There's a tube

sticking out of my leg. And what's this? Good Lord it's a grenade!"
There was indeed a grenade-shaped object attached to the other end of
the tube. It was made of blue translucent plastic and was half full of a
pink fluid, which had little flakes floating around in it. It reminded me
of pink lemonade with the pulp left in.

"A grenade is exactly what we call it." Laughed the doctor.
"It's handling the drainage of the fluid build-up in your leg."

"How long will I have that?" I asked.

"Until this is healed up." He said, as he exposed the wound on
my inner thigh.

It was a jagged vertical seam about eight inches long and a little
too close to the old groin area if you ask me, but of course nobody did.

"It may feel a little odd, kind of tight." The doctor said. "An
artery and a nerve were exposed as a result of the surgery. I had to pull
muscle tissue over to cover and protect them before we closed it up."

To me, it looked and felt like a trench had been dug in my leg
and then someone had taken a fistful of flesh from each side of the
trench, stretched it across the divide and held it together while someone

else made big wrap-around stitches to keep it closed. Not a pretty picture is it? That's what I'm trying to say.

"At least it's not a big *gaping* wound like the one I've got on my calf." I said without much conviction. "Now that we know the rest of those lymph nodes are clean, why don't you just put everything back the way it was? Then I won't have to worry about lymphedema." I was joking of course. I could do that now. They were clean! Nothing showed on my scans or in my blood! No satellite tumors. "Texas" really was a lone star!

There was no reason *not* to be optimistic. I could deal with lymphedema; a little fluid build-up in my leg? Fluid schmuid. Shoot, I could deal with that standing on my head. Hey, there you go! If I stood on my head often enough, fluid wouldn't be *able* to build up in my leg now would it? No, it wouldn't. Gravity. Maybe I had just come up with my own natural remedy for this lymphedema thing, which seemed to cause the doctor so much concern. Metastatic melanoma? Stage three? Stage left! I'm outa here! I've got a failing business to run after all.

THERE'S NO BUSINESS LIKE NO BUSINESS

Just before Christmas one of my drivers quit because he didn't want to drive through Pennsylvania in the snow any longer. Pennsylvania was one of the states we hauled to regularly. Isn't a truck driver a truck driver all year? I guess not, although I always thought so. I know I was.

I decided to look at it as an opportunity to put the driver I had been paying to sit home, back behind the wheel. He *wanted* to work. About this same time I was informed that the wrecked truck was repaired and ready to go. That was good news except that I no longer had a driver for that truck. We had to let the guy who wrecked it go. Our insurance carrier paid to fix the truck without raising our rates *only* if we terminated the driver. There were eyewitnesses on record who all gave statements to the police to the effect that they saw *our* driver run a red light and pull out in front of the oncoming vehicle. That's just nuts. He had to go whether the insurance company wanted him to or not. I'm just thankful no one was hurt.

We ran an ad for a driver but didn't have many applicants right before the holidays. I wasn't surprised. The few who did apply had, shall I say, less than exemplary driving records, which probably accounts for their availability.

The long and short of it is: We were paying for three trucks but only one was on the road. One had no driver and one was still down because of the transmission debacle. At this time we were still pursuing *that* mess, trying to get the outfit in North Carolina to make good on its work. I decided to jump in the truck that was just sitting. I thought maybe I could pull us out from under. By the end of that week my leg had swollen to twice the size of the other one and was stinging so badly from the pressure of the fluid build-up, that I couldn't go a second week.

I postponed the appointments to the oncologist and the lymphedema clinic that the vascular surgeon's office had made for me because I didn't have the slightest notion of how I would pay them. My medical costs were so high that I had to buy a twenty-four-foot extension ladder just so I could put any new bills I received on the top of the pile! My business and personal bills were piling up now too. Everything seemed to be getting out of hand at an exponential rate. Kathy tried to find work. She had no time before. She was running the business and running to the hospital, and taking care of me when I returned home. I tried to drive again. This time I didn't last three days. That's when I decided that I'd better go online and research this condition known as lymphedema. There was a button I could click on to see pictures of lymhedema in the advanced stages, so I clicked it. Good grief, *that* sobered me up and made me take it seriously! There was a photo of someone who had this affliction in their leg, just like me. It looked like an elephant leg! It was at least five times the size of the other leg and the foot was so fat the toes all pointed down, with the top of the toenails facing forward exactly like an elephant's! I realized right then and there that I would never be driving a big truck again.

We started putting our assets on the market, including the home that we so dearly loved. Financially, we were finished. The hardest part was facing it. The one positive, and a very important one at that, was that the cancer was all gone. At least that's what we thought.

TEARS OF A CLOWN

I finally did see the oncologist. He said that normally after a tumor like mine is removed they start the patient on an interferon therapy immediately. In my case however it had been about eight weeks since my surgery. The doctor said he had no data on whether or not an interferon would have any effect after so long. This is the first I had heard of the interferon business. Why hadn't somebody told me that was the normal procedure after the surgery? (I know you don't have the answer, dear reader, I'm just throwing the question out there.) The oncologist sent me for more scans and blood work, and said that if the results of *those* didn't show anything there would probably be no further treatment.

A week or so before my follow-up appointment, I developed what I believed to be a small cluster of heat blisters on my left thigh. That's right, the same leg. There were five of them. They were red on the surface and they stung whenever I accidentally scratched one of them with my fingernail. Actually, they stung when I did it on purpose too. They were each about the size of a "BB". I was concerned of course, but during the examination with the oncologist I pointed them out and he didn't think they were of much significance. My scans and blood work looked good again this time around so I quit worrying about the heat blisters.

On this same visit the doctor decided that he wanted a second opinion on the interferon treatment and I agreed to go to see a melanoma specialist at a leading university medical center.

In the time between the oncologist visits Kathy pursued, and succeeded in obtaining, medical benefits for me through Medicaid. I honestly didn't believe I could get them. Of course I had to be the next thing to a pauper before I was eligible, but I'm not complaining! Since my leg was still twice the size of the other one and frequently very painful, I made an appointment with the lymphedema clinic in South Bend to see their specialist, Dr. Klauer.

Dr. Klauer examined my leg, shark-bite and all, and said he thought I could benefit from their therapy, but he was concerned about the "heat blisters" on my thigh. He suggested I have them biopsied. I told him the oncologist didn't seem to be concerned about them but, since I had an appointment to see the melanoma specialist at the university, I would ask him about them.

"Make sure you do." Dr. Klauer said.

About a week later I was at the university medical center. The doctor there looked over my history, scan results, blood work, surgeries, etc. I had provided him with all that on a CD I had brought with me. He agreed that to start me on an interferon treatment at this late date would probably be of no benefit to me and may never have been in the first place. During the physical examination I casually pointed out the nodules on my thigh.

"That looks like melanoma." He said.

"No, no." I said. We're pretty sure that those are just heat blisters or something."

"Who is 'we'?" He asked.

I said, "Well . . .me, the oncologist, my wife . . "

"Is that right. I'm telling you this looks like melanoma. I'm going to have a couple of lab techs come in here and take a sample. I'll be back." He left the room and soon two young men came in and poked around on my little red bumps with some sort of special needles, and then they were gone. I was thinking this was an awful lot of fuss over a few little heat bumps on my leg, but I had an uneasy feeling. The doctor's brusque "bedside manner" had, no doubt, contributed to my unease. He returned.

"That *is* melanoma." He announced. I didn't know what to say.

"Are you sure?" I managed.

"The pathologist just finished looking at it under a microscope. I couldn't be *more* sure."

"Yes, but just a brief look under a microscope? Shouldn't we wait for the rest of the testing to be done?" I knew there must be some mistake.

"The rest of the testing? What further testing do you think there is? The pathologist who just looked at the sample has been at this for twenty some years. If he says it's melanoma, it's melanoma. You *do* know your melanoma had already metastasized, that it's stage three?"

"Yes." I said.

"Did they explain stage three to you?"

"Yes, they did." I said. "And I researched it on the internet."

"Well then, you know it's almost always fatal, correct?" The way he was regarding me, I actually expected him to say, "Duh!"

"It might have been mentioned a time or two." I said. "So . . . what do we do now?"

He described a surgery called degloving. "Basically all the tissue will be removed from your leg, much the same way in which the original tumor was handled, only now we're talking about the whole leg."

"You mean I won't have any skin at all left on my leg?" I looked around the room. Everything was hazy. The only thing that was in focus in the whole room was that doctor's face. And it was crystal clear.

"You'll have grafts." He said. "A plastic surgeon will take grafts from your back and your buttocks. It's major surgery. The risk of infection is quite high. You'll want to come back here for *our* plastic surgeon. I doubt if there is even anyone in your area *qualified* to perform this procedure. That is, of course, if we actually *do* the surgery."

"Why wouldn't we?" I asked. His eyes met mine. I thought for sure the "Duh!" was coming now.

"I wouldn't be at all surprised," he said, looking away, "if the melanoma had already traveled to your organs before we have a chance to *schedule* the procedure, much less perform it."

"And if it did?" I knew, but I wanted to be wrong.

"You told me you had researched this." He said.

"I have, but I want you to tell me there is something else."

"What I *can* say," he replied. "is that you will probably, at this point in time, want to make sure your affairs are in order. Now, if you'll stop by the front desk, they will set up an appointment for you to come back for scans, blood work, etc. Then we'll make the final determination concerning the surgery. We should waste no time here." We shook hands like we had just agreed on a lunch date, and he was gone.

The appointment they made was for three weeks out. I told the lady that the doctor wanted to get right on this thing as soon as possible. She said three weeks *was* as soon as possible.

I was walking down the hospital corridor, on my way out, when the doctor suddenly appeared as if he had stepped right out of the wall. I knew he had actually emerged from a doorway, but that's how badly tunneled my vision was at that point. He spoke. "I'm sorry I had to give you such bad news." So he *did* realize how he had sounded.

"I appreciate your saying that." I replied. "I was just walking down the hallway trying to convince myself this was all a bad dream. Thank you for bringing me back to reality. You are very good at that you know."

It was a three-hour drive to get back home to Kathy. I had told her I would call and let her know how things had gone. I couldn't do it. I thought I would be calling to joke with her like the clown I had always been. But as I pulled out onto the highway to head back home that day I could barely focus on the road, let alone that little keypad on the telephone. Besides, I'm sure I've read somewhere, in the literature that came with the phone maybe, that tears and electronics don't mix.

Kathy called *me* on my trip home that day and naturally she knew something was wrong. She seemed so far away. I just wanted to get home. I promised to be careful and then after we had hung up I thought about getting killed in some bizarre traffic accident. Wouldn't *that* be ironic! After all, I had driven a tractor/trailer over the road for thirty-one years and millions of miles without so much as a scratch (stab wounds not withstanding).

BLESSINGS FROM THE PAST

When I arrived home, Kathy came outside to greet me and, as usual, our hundred-pound black labrador, Elvis, was with her. He was considerably faster than Kathy and when he reached me he began happily running circles around me. I knelt down and ruffled his fur, holding his big head in both my hands. Most dogs won't look a person in the eye for very long when they are face-to-face and Elvis is no exception. This time however, he did. He settled down just briefly, his sincere brown eyes looking directly into mine as if to say, *You're home now. Everything's normal here. You're safe.* Then Kathy reached me and I straightened up and took her into my arms. Elvis, being the jealous goofball that he is, began jumping straight up into the air as if he were on a pogo stick.

We sat on the canopied swing (Kathy and I, not Elvis) and gazed out over the dazzling colors of Kathy's lovingly maintained flower garden. We held each other while I related my experience at the university medical center. Elvis was off sniffing the grass where a squirrel or rabbit had probably passed through while he was in the house. He looked around, and then up into one of the big oak trees, made a half-hearted, "Wuf," then came over and lay in the grass near the swing.

"You know, you should tell the kids about this." Kathy said, leaning her head against my shoulder.

"I know, I know." I said, dreading the thought.

"They can get pretty upset if they're left out in the dark for very long." I knew she was right.

"It just seems selfish on my part to cause them to worry any sooner than they need to. Right now, for instance, they are all at their jobs, or doing whatever they're doing, and they are thinking about other things, not worrying about this. In other word, they're living their lives. I feel like I would be shattering that peace of mind." Elvis looked up at me, then put his head back down on his paws. He tried briefly to watch me from that position but succumbed to a pair of heavy eyelids.

"What if it were one of them, or me, instead of you? You would want to know right away. If you were left out of the loop you wouldn't have the option of spending more time with them." She looked directly into my eyes. "If the worst thing happens here, won't you want to see them more often before . . . you know." I put my arm around her.

"I know you're right." I said. "I guess part of my problem with telling anybody else is that the more people I confide in, the more I am admitting the reality of it all to myself."

Kathy hugged me tightly and said, "Do you know what we're forgetting?"

"What's that?" I said, smelling the sweetness of her hair.

"The nuns!" She exclaimed. There was new enthusiasm in her voice. "You must still have some of those blessings left over!" And of course she was right.

What Kathy was referring to was something that had happened several years earlier when I had a part-time chimney cleaning business in addition to my tanker-driver job at Amoco Oil.

I received a call to go out to Notre Dame Avenue in South Bend to clean the fireplace chimney on a big old two-story house. Now this house happened to be the retirement home of a couple of dozen elderly nuns. The youngest of the bunch was probably in her late sixties. I'll call her sister Mary. Sister Mary was in charge of the day-to-day maintenance of the house and grounds. I guess she could reasonably be referred to as the building manager. She is the one who had called me. She told me it had been several years since the fireplace chimney had been cleaned. I set up my equipment and, as with most real masonry fireplaces, the flue could easily be cleaned from the bottom. There was no need to go up on the roof at all. I was glad of that because this roof was high and steep, and it had just begun to rain. The time of year was late autumn.

I cleaned the fireplace and chimney, sucking up all the soot and ashes with my specially designed vacuum. When finished, I began loading my equipment back into my van, trying to keep dry. To this day I have no idea why I did what I did next. I looked up into the battleship-gray, late-afternoon sky, and at the glistening wet slate of the roof, and decided I had to go up there.

The height of the roof required the use of my longest extension ladder. I had to secure it to the eave with a bunji cord because the wind was picking up and I didn't want the ladder to be blown down, leaving me stranded up on that roof with my ladder lying impotently on the ground. I was thoroughly soaked as I stood at the top of the ladder preparing to go on up. The sky appeared to have the potential to toss a few lightening bolts if it got the hankerin and my ladder was aluminum, not a good combination. Why was I doing this? I didn't really think about "why" at the time. I just did it.

It was slippery up there, and dark. In my memory it seems to have been nighttime, but I know it was between four and five pm. I held on to the edge of the roof with one hand as I climbed the steep incline to the peak. Once there, I didn't have to worry about sliding back down and I could get my bearings. I could see both the fireplace chimney and the furnace chimney. The furnace chimney is what held my interest. I carefully made my way over to it. The rain became heavier and I could hear the distant rumble of thunder. I was glad I had on a baseball cap, it kept the water from running into my eyes. My clothes were plastered to my body. The chimney was about four feet out from the roof peak and as I balanced myself there on that huge inverted "V", the top of the chimney was about a foot higher than the top of my head. *Great!* That meant that I couldn't shine my flashlight down the flue without actually climbing up on top of the chimney itself. I managed to get both hands onto the crown of the chimney by leaning out beyond the point of no return and was now standing at an angle with my feet on the peak of the roof and my hands and chest pressed up against the rough wet brick of the chimney. I pushed off with my feet and at the same instant I pulled myself up until I could get a knee on top the chimney. Then I pulled the rest of myself up there and crouched over the gaping black hole that was the mouth of the chimney flue. I brought the light forward out of my back pocket and shined it down the monster throat.

What I saw was approximately twenty feet down and no, it wasn't tonsils. There was a clog just like I knew there would be. The terra cotta tile, which lined the flue, had collapsed and had fallen down upon itself. It was an old, old chimney and the interior of it had never been protected from the elements with the simple installation of a chimney cap. I had seen this many times before but it was usually after a furnace repairman had advised the customer to have their chimney inspected because he had found the upward draft to be weak. *How did I know about this one?*

It probably took me a full half an hour to get back down from the roof without breaking my neck. When I did, I informed sister Mary of the clog in the furnace chimney and asked her if any of the sisters had complained recently of headaches or nausea, or both.

"Why yes." She said. "Several of the sisters, including myself, have had the most dreadful headaches just lately, and a few cases of nausea, some to the point of vomiting. We thought we were all coming down with some sort of flu-bug."

I said, "Sister, those are signs of carbon monoxide poisoning. We need to get the doors and windows of this place opened up so it can air out. I'll shut down the furnace and get that chimney unclogged." While sister Mary set about giving instructions to any other sister who happened to be within sight, I went outside and began bringing my equipment back in.

Sister Mary came down into the basement as I was spreading my drop cloth.

"You don't mind if I see do you?" she asked.

"No. Of course not." I said. I was just about to remove the furnace pipe from the hole in the masonry chimney. As I pulled it away, some crumbled bits of flue tile fell onto my drop cloth, but not much. The six-inch round hole was so packed with debris that there wasn't much room for movement.

"Oh my!" said sister Mary. "Could you wait just a moment please before you begin? Some of the other sisters are going to want to see this!" And they did.

One by one, the sisters who were spry enough, shuffled down the stairs to see what could very well have been, in just the next couple of days, the death of them all.

I removed buckets of the crumbled terra cotta liner from that flue and lugged every bit of it up the stairs and outside the house. When I was finished and coming up from the cellar for the last time, I was greeted by a gauntlet of elderly nuns from the top of the basement steps, down the hall, and all the way to the back door in the kitchen, outside of which my van was parked. As I passed between them, each of these gentle souls smiled and either delicately shook my hand, or patted me heartily on the back and gave me her own very heartfelt blessing:

"God bless you young man."

"Thank you and bless you."

"Bless you always."

"Thank you. Thank you so very much. And bless you."

"Our blessings be with you young man."

"Peace be with you always. And bless you."

This continued all the way out the door as I thanked each of them in turn and assured them that anyone would have done the same. I was so hot with embarrassment that I think my thoroughly drenched cloches dried on the spot.

When I stepped out onto the enclosed back porch sister Mary was waiting there with a huge office-style checkbook.

"I know what you charge for cleaning the fireplace chimney." She said. "We spoke of that on the phone. But what do we owe for the other? And please don't undercharge."

"I can't take any additional money for that, sister."

"But you *must* be paid for your time." She insisted. "You have been here almost five hours and most of that time was spent on the furnace chimney."

"Well sister," I said. "I think I *have* been paid. I must have been blessed enough in there to last me a lifetime." I looked back at the door and there they were, smiling back at me, waving with dainty little finger flutters. I turned back to sister Mary.

"I can't do it sister." I said. "I don't know what made me go up on that roof and check out your furnace flue. But sister, I *do* know that I had to do it. It was like I was being *lead* up there and well, if I took money for that part of my visit here, it just wouldn't be right." The sister studied me for a moment and then began writing in the checkbook. She ripped the check free and handed it to me. It was for the original amount we had agreed upon.

"May I add my blessing to those you've already received." She said. "And may these blessings always be with you."

"Right back at you!" I said, and she laughed.

I had no idea at the time, just how valuable all those blessings would later become to me. They would become one of the many reasons I would find in my life to have hope, and there is nothing more positive and more necessary than hope, in *all* our lives.

TRIP TO CANADA

For the next couple of days I spoke to all of the kids and informed them of the latest. Whoever happened to stop by, I told in person. The others I spoke to on the phone. There was great concern, and a few tears, but they were all optimistic, which is what I wanted, and needed.

I mean shoot, I could do without the skin on my left leg, couldn't I? Well sure I could! I hadn't been planning on wearing shorts anymore anyway, what with the shark bite and all. The trouble was - and this I hadn't shared with them - I had discovered five more nodules on my leg just since seeing the doctor at the university. They were just like the first five. I had no doubt about what they were. I made another appointment with the oncologist in my town right away and Kathy went with me to see him.

I showed the oncologist all ten nodules and reminded him that five of them had been there when last I'd seen him and he hadn't been very interested in them. He coughed up some baloney about how he knew I was going to see the university doctor anyway . . . I don't think he knew, or even thought, it might be melanoma popping back up.

I told him about the surgery the other doctor had prescribed as the only viable option. I asked him if there was anyone here, in our neck of the woods, qualified to do it. I told him what the university doctor had said about that and how he had said I would need to come back down there, which I really didn't want to do. The oncologist agreed that there probably wasn't anyone in our area qualified, and then said he needed to call the university medical center and speak to the melanoma specialist I had seen. He left the room to make the call. Kathy and I looked at each other uneasily. This business was making us both very nervous. I mean this *doctor* seemed to be nervous, so how else *could* we feel? When he returned to the examining room he looked worried, *that* was comforting.

"I couldn't reach him. He's on vacation." He announced. That explained why the university doctor's office wasn't able to schedule my next appointment for sooner that three weeks out.

Kathy said, "What are we supposed to do? This stuff is spreading. We can't just sit back and wait."

"No. No, we can't. Wait just one more moment. I'll be right back." He left again. Kathy's eyes met mine. I shrugged. What could I say? Soon he was back.

"I called the university again." He said. "I spoke to one of the doctor's colleagues. He reminded me that there is a doctor over at the Goshen cancer center who might be able to help you. Goshen, Indiana was only forty minutes away, but I didn't know anything about the "the Goshen cancer center".

"So the university can't help me?" I asked. "They already have all my records and everything."

"Well, with the one doctor on vacation and unable to see you, I think this is a viable option. I think you need to see *somebody*." Kathy was *not* a happy camper.

"Who tells someone that they have a life-threatening condition and that *theirs* is the *only* place around that can perform the surgery, and then goes on vacation! Who *does* that!" I felt like I was being stuffed into a very small box where I knew the air was going to run out.

"Would you like my staff to set up an appointment with the doctor in Goshen?" asked the oncologist, looking more than just a little ruffled.

"Yeah, sure." I said. "Thanks." I was thinking, *This guy's an oncologist - a cancer doctor - but what does he actually do?* Except for referring me to other doctors, I couldn't' think of a thing, and now he was handing me off to someone else like a hot potato. He wasn't cheap either.

The staff member who set up the appointment in Goshen told me the name of the doctor I would be seeing was Dr. Douglas Schwartzentruber. The appointment was for six days hence.

"Why so long?" I asked.

"That's the best I could do." She said.

"At least you have an appointment *somewhere*." Kathy said, taking my hand. "We've got to get going on this thing as soon as we can." I agreed of course. But now what would we do for the next six days? Play "connect the dots" with my little red bumps?

I had trouble sleeping that night. I had trouble sleeping *most* nights since this whole business began, but that night I didn't sleep at all. I lay there thinking about my family and how much I would miss them. I didn't know if it was possible to miss anyone after you died, but it didn't matter. Just thinking about the prospect made me miserable with longing for them, wishing I had been a better husband, dad, brother, nephew, uncle, friend.

Elvis came in and put his big black head on the bed beside me. Kathy was sleeping, though fitfully. I scratched Elvis's forehead and looked into those innocent brown eyes.

"Yeah, I know." I told him. "I miss you already too." Then tears suddenly began to just spill from my eyes as if they were waiting in little buckets that I hadn't known about. I seemed to have no control over this. I couldn't make it stop. I was glad Elvis was the only witness to this "carrying on". I knew I could trust him not to tell anyone.

The next morning I informed Kathy that we were going to Canada. I knew she wouldn't object. Her family is there. I thought she might need them right about then, and, truth be told, I did too. There were many of them that I had come to care deeply about over the years, to love, actually. Besides the fact that we both needed to absorb some of their strength, I was afraid this might be my last chance to see them. When I said this to Kathy she didn't disagree.

Since our youngest son, Ryan, still lived with us, he would be able to take care of Elvis in our absence, along with his own little dog Kobe (Pronounced: Koby). Ryan was working full-time so he couldn't go with us to Canada himself on such short notice.

The moment we arrived in Kitchener, Ontario I knew we had done the right thing. Kathy's dad and his wife, Ken and Joyce, greeted us with lots of smiles and hugs as usual. We just sort of hung out at their house, visiting with any friends or family who happened by. Ken and Joyce told us of all the prayers that had been coming our way from north of the border (more positive energy). They have a very strong relationship with their church and have given us thoughtful guidance many times in the past. On this visit, they gave me a book to read entitled: *Finding The Still Point* and written by Canadian author, Tom Harpur.

He writes about finding a balance within your own spirituality through meditation, contemplation, and prayer, and he writes from a Christian perspective. I knew I needed *something* in regard to my spirituality. Balance sounded about right.

On the title page of the book was this inscription from my in-laws:

Chuck & Kathy

We pray that you will continue the search for, and come to know, moment by moment, the constant comfort of the presence within you of the Holy Spirit of the creator God of us all, in life that is joyfully eternal.

Ken & Joyce

July 16, 2005

Those words, "the presence within you", started a new chain of thought in my mind and I took many things away from the reading of this book. I've never considered myself to be a particularly religious person, but I do, absolutely, believe in God. I know, for instance, that both good and evil forces exist, are constantly at battle, and that good is, without question, the stronger. I've always said that if you remove an "O" from the word good, you have God, and conversely, God *is* goodness. I also believe, as it says somewhere in Tom Harpur's book, that God is not just all around us, but within us. I believe the very spark of life that is the essence of each of us, is indeed God. Knowing that goodness is already within each of us, at the level of our soul, means to me that evil can only enter if *allowed* to enter. Therefore it can only be the weaker force.

I think the most useful thing I took away from this book at that particular time was the step-by-step instruction on how to meditate. I had never before meditated with any kind of structure or, for that matter, on purpose. Of course we have all "sat and thought a while" but, trust me, it's not the same thing. You can't get in touch with your essence, your own soul, your direct link to the infinite power of goodness, God, by simply thinking about it. You have to be able to leave all the physical aspects of yourself and ascend to the spiritual level.

Because of an example of a breathing exercise Tom Harpur shares in *Finding The Still Point*, I am now able to imagine myself afloat on a large log raft (modified from imagining you actually are a ship) adrift at sea. Each time I inhale deeply I rise on my raft with the swell of a great wall of water. When I exhale, my raft and I glide gracefully to the floor of the massive valley between swells. I find this to be extremely relaxing and can feel the tension leaving my body as if there were millions of tiny ghosts evacuating through my pores. I feel lighter than dandelion fluff floating off through a meadow, as light as a thought.

People speak of having "out of body" experiences. That is exactly what you are doing when you contact the bit of God within you, your own soul, through meditation.

I have to admit however, the concept of leaving my body does frighten me to a certain degree. Kathy says I'm forgetful and it would be just like me to misplace myself.

MONIKA

I was sitting in Ken and Joyce's living room speaking with Joyce and her neighbor, Rita. Rita is a nurse and we were discussing my melanoma thing when she mentioned an elderly German lady named Monika who is a spiritual healer. It seems that Rita had been having some pretty severe back pain and, even with her extensive access to conventional medical resources, she was unable to find relief. I don't remember how Rita was introduced to Monika, but apparently Rita's back pain was a thing of the past as a result of her visits with Monika. She couldn't say enough good things about her.

Rita asked me if I would like her to find out if Monika would see me. What could I say? No thanks. I'd rather not try absolutely anything and everything that might have even the most remote chance of saving my life. Of course I said yes!

At this point we had been in Canada a couple of days and my ten nodules had become fifteen. I was open to virtually anything. Monika works with the spiritual realm. Wasn't my spiritual side actually my soul? Hadn't I been trying to do, essentially, the very same thing on my own, through meditation? We are all spiritual beings having a human experience, right?

That evening Rita called Joyce and said Monika would see me right away so Joyce, Kathy, Rita, and I all loaded ourselves into Rita's van and away we went. We arrived at Monika's at about 9:pm. I though to myself, *What a nice lady, to see a perfect stranger at such a late hour, and on such short notice.* Ok, I'm not so perfect, but I *was* a stranger.

Monika lives on a farm out in the middle of somewhere (by definition, "nowhere" does not exist). Her friend Hildegard was there with her when we arrived. Hildegard was to be Monika's interpreter should she need one. Monika speaks English but not as well as Hildegard and she wanted to be sure nothing was left unsaid or misunderstood.

Rita made introductions all around and then each of us took a seat at the big wooden table in Monika's spacious kitchen. Monika was maybe five feet four inches tall with gray hair and a friendly, but no-nonsense, way about her. After I had answered a handful of questions from her, she got down to business. From somewhere, she produced a pendant on a chain. She held the chain with one hand, letting the pendant dangle at the end of it as she passed it slowly over all areas of my body. She paused briefly over my stomach and let the pendant swing there a moment until it stopped and began to move in small circles. Then she wrote something on a pad of paper before continuing.

The next place the pendant paused and began to circle was over my left leg. Her eyes met mine.

"This is where big trouble is." she said. She wasn't asking, she knew.

"Yes." I said. "That's where the cancer is." She made some more notes.

"I ask for advice now, and wisdom from spiritual side." She said. Monika closed her eyes for several moments and then, without opening them, began to scribble frantically on a blank sheet of paper. As we watched, the hand with the pencil in it started jumping all over the paper, seemingly taking its direction from someone other than Monika. I don't know what anyone else was thinking at the time, but I was fascinated. Here I was, somewhere out in the country, in the general vicinity of Kitchener, Ontario, Canada, inside a big beautiful farmhouse, experiencing something of which I had only seen the likes on television.

Frankly, I had never taken this kind of thing seriously, but there is something about Monika that feels genuine and honest. Remember, she didn't know me from Kevin (I know, everyone else uses Adam) before that evening, and she wasn't doing this for money. As a matter of fact, before we left I asked her if I could give her something for her trouble. She said no. She said she could not take payment for using her "gift". This gift was part of her family heritage. Her father had it while he was living, and when he passed on Monika acquired it. The gift is to be used to help others while on this physical plain, not for personal profit.

My understanding of Monika's "gift" is that she has the ability to ask for, and then hear, advice from the spiritual realm. Monika told me that there is a place in my house where I spend a lot of time, and where there is a source of radiation, which is affected by a magnetic field of water flowing beneath my feet. These things combine in such a way that negative energy is generated and radiated outward. Anything else of a negative nature that was going on with me physically, was fed and helped along by this "bad" energy.

The place Monika was speaking of was my home office, specifically, my computer desk. The water she mentioned flowing under my feet threw me for just a second, but then I remembered what an elderly gentleman down the street had told me just after we had moved in to our house. He said there is an underground river that flows beneath the whole neighborhood and as a result, nobody "in these parts" has ever had any trouble with their well going dry.

Monika had no way of knowing that. Come to think of it, she had no idea which leg had the cancer either - I didn't have a limp or anything at the time - but she told me just the same. Remember the pendant pausing over my stomach and beginning its slow circling? Sure you do. Well, I've had what I thought was this acid reflux problem for years and, if I didn't eat a ton of Rolaids, I was sure I was going to have a serious hole burned right through my esophagus. Monika told me there was a form of bacteria in my stomach and she told me what to do about it using a natural remedy. I can't pass on her words here because someone might construe them as medical advice and we all know how litigious our society is these days. It's a shame. I will say this however: This same natural remedy can be found on the internet with a little diligent research. I know, I checked.

Back to my leg (I do get sidetracked don't I?) Monika told me what I could do to change the negative energy in my house. By the way, she drew a rectangle representing a rough sketch of my house and showed me where the nearest electrical transformer is. She was correct. She's a pretty cool lady. What she said next is what I remember most.

I had told her about my appointment with a new doctor when I returned home. She touched my pant leg over the spot where the original tumor had been and said, "This one is gone. Will not come back. Is no more trouble. These new things, what you have?" She pointed toward my thigh.

"Yes?" I responded.

"This new doctor will help. He will know what to do." She said.

"Are you sure?" I asked.

"I contact your soul." She said, matter-of-factly. I was almost speechless (but then I *am* me after all).

"You what? You contacted my soul?" I didn't even try to hide my surprise. She nodded.

"Yes, I contact your soul." I quickly pulled myself together.

"Well I'm glad you found one to contact." I joked. Everyone got a chuckle out of that, including Monika. Until now she had been pretty serious, no expression of any kind on her face. She was smiling now as she said,

"I find soul who is not ready to go anyplace yet, very *strong* soul. Has much more work to do here."

"That is really good to hear." I said sincerely. I looked at Kathy. She had tears in her eyes.

"I would tell you." Monika said very seriously. "If it was the other way, soul not so good. I would tell you, help you prepare."

"Thank you." I said. "I know you would."

Before we left Monika's house that evening she gave us a tour of the place. She was obviously very proud of all the work her late husband had done. He was a master craftsman from "the old country" and it showed everywhere, from the massive hand-hewn timbers in the vaulted ceilings, to the great stones set into the hearth of the huge fireplace, each by hand, she assured us. I'm about as handy as a wheelbarrow with legs, so I was honestly in awe.

This visit to Canada, and to Monika's, took place in July 2005 and, just like back home in northern Indiana, Kitchener, Ontario had been suffering through a lengthy dry spell. I remember Hildegard commenting to Joyce at some point in Monika's kitchen that Monika was worried about her crops, with all the dry weather. Sitting in one of the rear seats of Rita's van as we were leaving that evening, I remember thinking to myself, *I hope this weather changes and Monika gets some rain for her crops.* I was feeling overwhelmingly grateful to Monika. She had invited me into her home and, as I've said, she didn't know me from Kevin. She wanted to do whatever she could to help me and I wanted to return the favor. Now I'm *not* saying I had anything to do with it, but the day we left Canada for home it started to rain, and it rained, and it rained. It rained for three days straight! Check it out at the library or somewhere. I know it was probably just another one of those odd coincidences, but it really did rain.

Believe what you will about faith healing and my experience

with Monika. All I know is that when I left there that night, I took with me something with which I had not arrived: A better feeling, a more positive mindset, like all was not lost. It was a source of positive energy that I couldn't deny, and that I badly needed.

When I thought about Monika saying she had contacted my soul, I thought, *Shouldn't I have felt something when she did that? Shouldn't it have maybe tingled a little at least?* But later I realized, through this whole ordeal with the cancer, that I didn't know beans about my own soul. Monika is a spiritual person. Why shouldn't she be able contact my soul? As far as I knew, I had never yet actually been in contact with it myself. Unfortunately, I probably wouldn't have recognized my own soul if it had walked up and kicked me in the butt. I guess that is, in essence, why I'm writing this book. Some people don't even acknowledge that they *have* a soul, let alone that it's their source for healing and their direct link to the infinite power of goodness. These folks need what I have obtained, what Kathy calls "soul awareness". I don't know where she heard that. It's possible that she made it up. There is such peace of mind in the discovery of your own soul - in soul awareness (Thanks Kathy) - but look what it took for *me* to realize all this. Maybe some lost soul out there will cause its physical self to pick up a copy of this book somewhere and reading it will help the two of them get together. Wouldn't that be something? To me it would. I'm trying to give something back here. Could *you* possibly be one of the many people out there who has a need to know your own soul? To believe it exists, to know beyond all doubt that this physical life isn't all there is? You can nod your head; I can't see you. I, my friend, have been on the threshold of the very door we have all wondered about in our most thoughtful moments. You'll see what I mean as you read on.

TWO BOOKS, ONE MESSAGE

On our trip to Canada we also visited Kathy's mother Judi, and her husband, Jim. It so happens that Jim also gave me a book he thought might be helpful. It was entitled *The Journey* and was written by a lady named Brandon Bays. This book is, amazingly enough, about tapping in to the healing power of your own soul.

Ms. Bays writes about a story she once heard wherein it is said that when a person is born, their soul is "flawless, pristine, brilliantly radiant, and perfect." Over the course of their life they keep dumping layer after layer of emotional garbage onto this pure and flawless gem. Then as adults they cover this bulging mess with a coat of "rosy" colored lacquer and it's this shiny veneer that they present to the world as "who they are". Ms. Bays describes how, beginning with meditation, a person can peel away all those layers of "crap" and expose to themselves that utterly beautiful stone that is who they really are, their essence, their soul, and, of course, the great spiritual healing power within.

I used a combination of the techniques I learned in both the Brandon Bays book and the Tom Harpur book, to begin shoveling away the sh__(stuff) that had piled up over *my* lifetime. The peace I found was . . . well, I'll tell you about that in a little while.

Right now, before I forget, I have to mention that being given these two books, each at this particular time, was too much of a coincidence to be a coincidence. They were both positive thinking, positive energy books. One had more of a Christian flavor to it than the other, but they were essentially about the same thing: Learning to make contact with your own soul through meditation so that you might tap into the "infinite wisdom", the "spark of God" that is there within all of us and use that "source" to help your body to heal itself. Interestingly enough, both books, I discovered, contained the same passage from a 1992 bestseller, *A Return to Love*, by Marianne Williamson. The authors of the two books that were given to me both apparently thought this passage summed up something they were each trying to convey. Remember: These two books were written by two different people, from different walks of life, different generations, and even different countries! Apparently I was suppose to read Marianne Williamson's words, and so are you, because here they are:

Our deepest fear is not that we are inadequate.

Our deepest fear is that we are powerful beyond measure.

It is our light, not our darkness, that most frightens us.

We ask ourselves, Who am I to be brilliant, gorgeous, talented,
and fabulous?

Actually, who are you not to be?

You are a child of God.

Your playing small doesn't serve the world.

There is nothing enlightening about shrinking

so that others won't feel insecure around you.

We were born to make manifest the glory of God

that is within us.

It's not just in some of us; it's in EVERYONE!

And as we let our own light shine, we unconsciously

give other people permission to do the same.

As we are liberated from our own fear,

our presence automatically liberates others.

Our visit in Canada wrapped up a couple of days earlier than we had planned because I had discovered that the fifteen melanoma nodules on my left leg had become at least twenty-five. I started feeling an urgent need to see this new doctor. The melanoma seemed to me to be multiplying exponentially. Although I knew that wasn't literally true, the anxiety I was experiencing from the new discovery made that fact irrelevant. I wanted to get home. I wanted to do whatever was needed to get this new doctor, this Dr. Schwartzentruber guy, to see me early. I was willing to go to his house, camp out in his driveway, mow his lawn, anything to get my appointment moved up.

It turned out that none of that was necessary. When we called that first day back from Canada Dr. Schwartzentruber's office said,

"Sure, how about tomorrow?" I'm thinking, *Geez, why didn't we call before we went to Canada?* Actually I knew why. After the last couple of experiences I'd had with doctors, why in the world would I expect one to see me early?

As I reflect on this now however, I think I was suppose to see those people in Canada. You see, whether they were family, as were Kathy's dad Ken and his wife Joyce, Kathy's brother Nigel and his family, her sister Alex, her mom Judi and her husband Jim, Jim's daughter Suzy and husband Rod, or whether they were friends and acquaintances, old or new, such as Rita, Monika, and Hildegard, everything I received from these loving people was positive. Positive energy. I needed that. Sure I had positive energy coming from my family here in the States, all five of our kids and their kids, my sisters Bea, and Brenda and her husband Jerry, and their families. God only knows what shape Kathy and I might have been in without *their* love and support. I think though, that I needed it all. Both sides of the family, the heart to heart talks, the experience at Monika's, the two books - different, but incredibly alike. Was all this just coincidence? You'll never convince *me* of that. I was touched so much by so many.

For instance when we arrived back home there was already an e-mail waiting for me from Jim Pedder's daughter Suzy, telling me how much she had been able to relate to the story of my experience at Monika's farmhouse, and of her sincere wishes and prayers on my behalf. This thoughtfulness came from a woman who has spent many years as the loving mother of an autistic little boy. She knows something of adversity and dealing with life's challenges. She also knows the joy that some of those God-given "duties" can bring. I see it in both Suzy and her husband Rod, and I admire them both more than they know for their strength.

As a matter of fact, Suzy's e-mail is what prompted me to write a letter of thanks to Monika for helping to open me to myself, which is really the most important thing she did. She started the ball rolling by causing me to recognize the literal existence and importance of my soul, which paved the way for the two books I was about to receive.

I wanted to thank everyone I'd seen in Canada but I was too lazy to write to each of them individually so I e-mailed a copy of the "Letter to Monika" to everyone. It was the response and approval I received about that letter that gave me the confidence I needed to begin this book.

DR. SCHWARTZENTRUBER

Kathy and I waited for Dr. Schwartzentruber to enter the room where I was already attired in one of those snazzy hospital gowns. All the proper forms had been filled out and my vital signs had been taken and duly recorded by Debbie, Dr. Schwartzentruber's nurse.

I was apprehensive. Shoot, I was nervous. How many times had I been told, or read on the internet, that stage three melanoma is "almost always fatal"? Was this new doctor going to be mostly just guessing about what to do as so many of the others seemed to be? Kathy was reading a brochure she had picked up downstairs in the lobby, which contained a short bio on the doctor. It seems he was with the National Cancer Institute in Bethesda, Maryland for some sixteen years where he was Senior Investigator. He established a melanoma research center in his hometown of Goshen, Indiana, and is coordinating a national clinical trial he initiated while at the N.C.I.

Hmm . . . Ok, that sounded pretty good. He was listed as Douglas J. Schwartzentruber, MD, FACS, Surgical Oncologist and Medical Director of The Center for Cancer Care at Goshen Health Systems. I'm thinking, *This guy's got to have twenty-five years or more of schooling! He must have a handle on this stuff!*

There was a knock on the door and the man who came in and introduced himself as Dr. Schwartzentruber was warm and friendly, but he didn't look old enough to have accomplished all those things. He looked as though he were maybe thirty-five or so. Quickly deducting the years of education I had already determined him to have had, I figured that he would have to have graduated from high school at the age of nine or ten! Could that be? Or was this man an imposter then? At one point when he left the room momentarily, I asked someone how old he was and she said she thought he was about forty-eight. That's more like it. He's closer to my age. Kathy thought I was awfully nosy, but I felt more at ease just the same.

I found Dr. Schwartzentruber to be very professional, genuinely caring, and at once likable. I told him what Dr. What's His Name at the university had said about the solution to the new tumors being the removal of all the remaining skin on my leg. After examining me thoroughly, Dr. Schwartzentruber said that was definitely *not* a remedy for my situation. He told me about a relatively new therapy that is sometimes effective on melanoma and a certain type of kidney cancer. He didn't pull any punches. He told me that the chance of the therapy being one hundred percent effective is about six percent. But he instilled confidence, and what he *didn't* say was that stage three melanoma "is almost always fatal". He knew there was hope and that the negative was not what I needed at this point.

The therapy is referred to as IL-2 therapy, which is short for interleukin-2. This is how I understand the therapy to work: Our bodies naturally produce interleukin-2 in small quantities. Interleukin-2 is a protein that activates our T cells and NK (natural killer) cells. The T cells and NK cells hunt and attack abnormal cells such as cancerous cells and attempt to destroy them. Interleukin-2 can now be genetically engineered making it possible to inject patients with massive doses, thereby activating more T cells and NK cells than normal. The genetically engineered form of interleukin-2 is actually called Proleukin and is interleukin-2 in its pure form. Because injecting a patient with interleukin-2 boosts their natural immune system it is referred to as an immunotherapy and it doesn't cause good cells to be destroyed along with the bad, as some of the more conventional treatments for cancer do. I liked the sound of that. Dr. Schwartzentruber took the time to make sure we understood the process, and that none of our questions went unanswered. We both felt good about this guy, like I was finally in good hands.

KISSING OUR BUTTS GOODBYE

Dr. Schwartzentruber wanted to get me started on the IL-2 therapy right away and, of course, I did too. There was one little problem though, a snag in the ointment, a fly in the stocking if you will. I was a smoker. Kathy and I both smoked. Dr. Schwartzentruber said I had to be free of cigarettes for a minimum of two weeks before beginning the IL-2. We scheduled the therapy for approximately seventeen days out. Exactly fourteen days before I was to be admitted, Kathy and I both quit smoking. I did it because I was given no choice. Kathy did it to make it easier on me. You see what I mean about this lady? She's my soul mate. I have that on good authority too by the way, since I have now been in contact with my soul. I guess it's time to talk about that.

I was having a heck of a hard time with the not smoking thing. As of this writing it has been ten months and I still get the craving from time to time. After all, I was thoroughly addicted. I had smoked for some thirty-five years. I've heard it said that nicotine is more addictive than heroin. I don't know if that's true and I'm not going to become a junkie and then quit cold turkey just to find out. I'm not that curious. I've never been that curious about drugs. I know they say if you can remember the sixties, you weren't there. Well, in case my kids or grandkids read this, I lived through the sixties and I remember them very well - for the most part.

Ok now, where was I? What's with this short-term memory loss nonsense? (Just kidding!)

We substituted Tootsie Pops for our cigarettes. It gave us a pacifier and something to do with our hands (So what if we have to buy a few teeth later on?). The suckers helped us to handle the psychological addiction, the habitual part of smoking. The physical addiction could only be overcome with the passage of time. Or so I thought.

I decided to try utilizing what I had learned from the two books I had received while in Canada. I had read most of the book Ken and Joyce had given me while I was still up there. I finished it upon returning home and immediately devoured the one given to me by Jim and Judi. I was determined to access my inner self, my source, my soul.

At least now, thanks to Monika, I was relatively confident there was something in there to access.

That night in bed, I made myself comfortable lying on my back and began the relaxing breathing exercise I'd learned from *Finding the Still Point*. I closed my eyes and began breathing deeply, seeing myself on my large log raft out at sea. With every breath I drew, I saw and felt myself rising to the top of a great swell. As I slowly released the air from my lungs, I descended to the bottom of these great walls of water. I saw an old sailing ship that reminded me of an artist's rendering of the early ships which were used to discover "the new world". The ship was very far off and as I endeavored to see nothing but the foaming deep green of the sea around me, the ship vanished. I remember thinking later, *I hope that wasn't my ship finally "coming in"* because if it was, I had managed to avoid it once again.

Once I had attained a totally tranquil state, I began to take myself inside my own body by envisioning it, following the guidelines of Brandon Bays in *The Journey*. First I saw in my mind my own face, which is an easy thing for anyone to do. Then I looked into the back of my throat and followed the air passage into my lungs. There was more pink in there than I had expected to find after having been a smoker for so long, but there were plenty of dark places too. Brandon Bays explored her own tumor in this way to try to rid her self of it, which she eventually did. I, on the other hand, was not trying to rid myself of my lungs. My plan was to envision them the way they were then, as a smoker's lungs, and then watch as all the dark spots slowly faded away, leaving behind the healthy, vibrantly pink color that they were supposed to be. It was pretty cool. I was this tiny little thing floating around in this massive cavern with its glistening wet walls and I actually saw them change color and become more alive. I'm glad nothing caused the big me to sneeze or hack anything up while I was in there!

That image of my lungs "pinking up" is what I rely on to get me past the physical craving for nicotine whenever it arises, and it definitely still arises, although less frequently all the time. I would like Kathy to try this technique too, to make it easier for her to resist the craving. She says she might, but who knows, maybe she won't need to.

Don't tell her I said this, but she's always been stronger than me, in many ways.

You may very well be thinking to yourself at this time, *If he's got all those melanoma tumor things on his leg, and he really believes this "healing with the help of your own soul" stuff, why doesn't he try it on the tumors, huh? Answer me that!* Well, I *did* try it on the tumors. I was getting to that. Let's exercise a little patience here, shall we? Thank you.

TAPPING THE SOURCE

A day or so before I went in for my first weeklong IL-2 therapy, they put me through a stress test for my heart. I had more scans and more blood work. They were checking to make sure nothing had shown up in my organs yet and my heart was tested because apparently this therapy was going to kick my butt. Dr. Schwartzentruber had to be as sure as he could be that my heart could handle it. Needless to say, it passed the test (Have you ever noticed how people will say, "Needless to say" and then they'll go right ahead and say it anyway?).

It was the night before my therapy began that I tried seeking help from within myself, from the core of my being, the source of all that I am, the power of infinite goodness, the spark of life that is the light of God . . . Gee, I guess I could have just said, "my soul".

By the way, one of the easiest ways to maintain my positive state of mind, which is essential for a positive result is, as I may have already mentioned, to keep my sense of humor. There have been times when I really had to dig deep to find it, but I am thoroughly convinced that the old adage, "Laughter is the best medicine." Is indeed the truth. Just the fact that this old saying became an "adage" lends credence to the whole thing, don't you think?

I mean, think about it. What must it take to even *become* an adage? Each of those five words – laughter is the best medicine - standing alone, are just words. Oh, they were important enough to actually become words in the first place, make no mistake about that. However, as a group, arranged in a particular order, they have been awarded "adage" status. Someone, at some time in the past, must have nominated them for the honor. Was a committee then formed to vote on the matter? Or was the issue offered up for public referendum? And think of all the unfortunate groups of words that must have been nominated but didn't cut the mustard. Was it enough for them just to have been nominated? I think not my friend. I think not. And don't even get me started on that little "cut the mustard" phrase up there!

I seem to have strayed from the subject just a tad here. Back to it then!

In *The Journey* Brandon Bays wrote about the need to get through all the layers of garbage we've built up over our lifetimes in order to finally reach our "source" and its healing power. The night before being admitted into the hospital for my first week of therapy, I attempted to do just that.

I was lying in bed, all was dark and Kathy had already drifted off to sleep. I closed my eyes and went drifting on my log raft as I had before. It didn't take me long to find that peaceful state of mind. I stayed in that tranquility and just let whatever wanted to come in to my mind, enter freely. I began to understand that the "layers" I had read about, and the memories of different traumatic experiences in my life, were one and the same.

As the memories came, I didn't try to ignore them or push them away. I let them wash over me one at a time and accepted them. No matter how unpleasant, hurtful, sad, or even shameful a memory might be, I didn't deny it. I'm sure you can see that if I had, I would have accomplished nothing. I would have been simply layering on more dishonest crap. Now that I understood that, there was no moral alternative. In other words, I could no longer lie to myself about anything.

As I descended deeper and deeper into myself, I saw a handful of memories that I would need to come back and deal with specifically some time soon. Especially the one that stood out the most and seemed to be buried the deepest. It was the memory of the evening in 1959 when my father had died suddenly at the age of twenty-seven. In the memory I was six years old and trying to get my "daddy" to let me go with him wherever it was that he was going. He told me that he was sorry but I couldn't go this time, and he was very firm about it. This I couldn't understand because he usually took me with him when he had an errand to run if I wanted to go. He even took my sister and me to work with him at the local Oldsmobile dealership on more than one occasion.

In the memory, I see him backing out of the driveway, driving down our street, and disappearing around the corner. That's the last time I saw him alive. He died of a heart attack that evening. My grandfather (his father) said he was sure my dad knew it was coming. He had confided in my grandpa about the heart condition sometime previously. It was the result of a wound he had received in Korea. We are all convinced that the reason he went away that evening was because he was suddenly aware that something was about to occur, and he didn't want it to happen at home in front of his wife and two small children. I remember my grandpa and grandma coming to our house that night and my grandpa taking my sister Brenda and me onto his lap and telling us our daddy had died. We cried and *he* cried, which made us cry all the harder. I remember having this overwhelming feeling that if I had just tried a little harder to get my dad to let me go with him that night, somehow things would have turned out differently. He would still be alive. I know of course that isn't true. My presence would have made no difference. At six years old however, anything was possible and I had this tremendous feeling of guilt that, "if only . . ."

I missed my dad terribly and for quite some time I cried myself to sleep each night after faithfully praying for God to "Please bring my Daddy back." We needed him much more than God did after all. I did this until finally one night my Mom came in to my room and demanded that I stop it. God was not bringing my Dad back. Nobody was. It was time I stopped this crying every night. She wasn't being cruel. She knew I had to face reality and I can only imagine what it must have done to her to listen to my pathetic pleading while trying to cope with her own loss.

At this writing, I have indeed dealt with this memory from childhood and in doing so have uncovered many others. My mother remarried you see, and the man she married didn't exactly look upon me as a blessing, or a son, or even a stepson for that matter. He never called me by my name. When he addressed me it was always as "boy". Kathy thinks that story should be my next book. She may have something there. We'll see. I may have already mentioned that Kathy is right much more of the time than I seem to be.

Back on point: The night before my first IL-2 therapy I meditated myself down through the layers of garbage, accepting each of them and letting them pass so that I could deal with what was happening then, the melanoma. Following the example of Brandon Bays again, I let my mind take me into my leg so that I could see all the nodules of cancer from that point of view. They looked much the same from this vantage point in my mind's eye, except that I could see them from the underside. It was as if I were suspended beneath the surface of the ocean and, looking up, I could see these round red buoys floating in clusters there on the surface. The very fact that I could see the underside of them confirmed my thinking, that they couldn't be deep (The original tumor on my calf had been *very* deep. It had penetrated every layer of tissue.). That gave me a tremendously positive feeling. There is a word for this feeling. Wait a moment. It's right on the tip of my typing fingers . . . Hope! That's it! Realizing that these melanoma nodules, although there were many more of them (some thirty by this time), couldn't possibly be as deep as the original, gave me great hope. Hope is a very positive and powerful thing. I began to envision the nodules getting smaller and fading away until, one by one, they were all gone.

When I physically opened my eyes and looked, and when I reached down and felt with my hand, the nasty little buggers were still there. Of course they were, but I had this tremendously positive feeling about what was going to happen the next day.

I should point out here that besides the powerful optimism of which I just spoke, I was also developing an inner peace regarding the whole dying business. I guess because the process of "tapping in" to the power of my own soul required that I believe I *have* a soul, it also caused me to consider and literally accept, some other basic spiritual truths: Good and evil *do* exist just as polar opposites exist, and just as light and darkness exist. Evil is everything negative and dark. Good is the positive, the spark of life. That spark is our essence, our soul, the light of goodness, or God. Because I see all this so clearly now, I am much more at ease with the idea of moving from this life to the next. In short, I'm not seeing everything backwards anymore as if I was spiritually dyslexic, and I'm not confused and constantly wondering about God like an agnostic. I am simply seeing the wonder. Gee, this kind of segues nicely in to a joke I once heard: Did you hear about the dyslexic, agnostic, insomniac? He lies awake all night wondering if there really is a doG.

INTERLEUKIN-2

(First Round)

In August of 2005 I was admitted into Goshen Hospital's Intensive Care Unit (ICU). It was a trifle strange because people don't usually enter the ICU under their own power. Here I was walking in, slipping on a gown, and climbing into my bed just like I knew what I was doing. I felt like I was cheating, like I had just parked in a "Handicapped" parking spot, not really needing it.

You would think the "Intensive Care Unit" would be a quiet place, wouldn't you? No such thing. Alarms went off from time to time, and because my curtain blocked my view more often than not, I could only *hear* all the different pairs of feet running to and fro out there as they rushed to one room or another to resuscitate or otherwise assist someone. (I assume all the running feet were in pairs; I don't know it to be fact.) As circumstances would have it, I was the only person in the ICU who was in any shape to care whether or not it was quiet. That was about to change. I had been told what to expect from the effects of the IL-2, but still, I had no idea.

There was a lot to do before I actually began receiving my "massive doses". Kathy and I met the day shift nurse who was assigned to me. Her name was Linda, and she was very courteous, professional, and helpful with all the questions that began popping into my head regarding what was about to happen to me. Linda was one of just a handful of ICU nurses who were trained and experienced in the care of IL-2 patients. As she took and recorded my vital signs, the reality of my situation began to sink in. Here I was, in the Goshen *Cancer* Center. The dreaded "C" word, and I was in *Intensive Care* to boot! Boot? Boot Hill. What made me think of that old western term? Oh, I knew what it was all right. People died here! It happened every day. No big deal. EXCEPT MAYBE TO ME!

I wasn't getting any of these panicky, fatalistic thoughts from Linda or Kathy. I was manufacturing them all by myself. As a matter of fact, it was the aura of competence surrounding Linda that gave me the confidence to vent these things I was feeling, and get back on a positive track. I didn't need any negative thoughts or worries if this Interleukin-2 stuff was going to do me any good. I knew that. I just needed to keep the proper perspective. I got a few chuckles out of Linda, and rolled eyes from Kathy, so I must have filtered my concerns through my sense of humor, and not let them get a glimpse of the paranoid lunatic I was harboring within.

After lots of questions and answers, flowing both ways, Linda informed me it was time to go and have my PICC line put in. She whipped back my curtain and, sure enough, there stood a lady with a wheelchair. Since she was already standing, I utilized a little deductive reasoning and figured out that the chair was for me. Amid mutual greetings, I seated myself and away we went.

"I could walk you know." I told the nice lady.

"I know you could." She replied pleasantly. "But the rules are the rules."

"I suppose so." I said. "And besides, think how cruel you would appear to be if you were pushing me down the hallway while I were *walking*."

She laughed. "Yes I do have my image to think about, don't I? Here we are."

The nice lady deposited me through a door, into a room where I appeared to be the only thing that was not sterile (of course in one sense I was: Back in 1981 I had a vas . . . well, never mind). This is where my PICC line would be installed. "PICC" stands for Peripherally Inserted Central Catheter. I knew that word "catheter" and I didn't like the sound of this already.

Another nice lady asked me to lie down on an adjustable padded-table-workbench-type-thing. She told me the PICC line was a catheter they would insert into a vein in my upper arm. *Whew!* I thought. That beat the heck out of where I thought it would be inserted! They would then push this tube slowly through my vein until it was just above my heart. This would then serve as the access point for all my medication, including the IL-2. There were four people involved in this procedure besides me. The first lady, who seemed to be in charge, wore a mask as did her assistant. The other two were in another room, sitting behind a large window where I presume they were monitoring some sort of instruments. It did cross my mind however, that the little room could be one of many possible places in a hospital where one might go for lunch and a show, but if either of the two on the other side of the window took a bite from a sandwich or a pull on a straw from a Slurpee, I didn't see it.

I asked the first masked lady if maybe I ought to be wearing a mask too, since I probably have my share of germs. Her response, although muffled, made sense. Apparently, even though the risk of infection is high while the PICC line is being inserted, the idea of my infecting myself with my own germs is, well . . . kind of silly.

The PICC procedure was handled with great efficiency and I was soon rolling through the corridors of the hospital again, heading back to my room in ICU. I hadn't really thought about it before, but the ICU is the one place in the hospital where you are virtually *guaranteed* a private room.

I was just getting settled back into my bed, when my nurse Linda magically reappeared.

"What's your date of birth?" She asked.

"One, seven, fifty-three." I said.

"What's your name?" She was smiling slightly.

"Uh, Linda, it's me, Chuck. We met about an hour and a half ago?"

"Do you know where you are?" She asked. I don't know how she kept a straight face.

"Linda, You're starting to worry me now. You're supposed to take care of me, and you don't even recognize me or know where we are?" She just looked at me, waiting.

"Ok." I said. "We're at The Center for Cancer Care, Goshen, Indiana." Linda was all smiles now.

"Good." She said. "That might seem silly, but pretty soon you are going to receive your first dose of IL-2. From that point on, you will periodically be asked these questions to determine if you are lucid, coherent."

Dr. Schwartzentruber came in to see me before ordering my first dose. He looked at my chart, listened to my heart and lungs, and examined my thirty-odd nodules again. We talked about what I could expect from the IL-2 as far as my body's initial reaction. We had spoken of these things before, but now it was time and Dr. Schwartzentruber, I think, was trying to instill in me as much confidence as possible.

He did. I honestly believed I couldn't be in better hands. Now, as I'm writing this, I *know* it was true. There is no false pretense about Dr. Schwartzentruber. He simply knows what he's doing, and he cares about his patients. It's really no more complicated than that. The Goshen Center For Cancer Care, which *is* Dr. Schwartzentruber as far as I'm concerned, promotes the philosophy that mind, body, *and* spirit all need to be healthy and in harmony. What a perfect place for me to be! I was trying to keep my mind healthy with positive input and a "medicinal" sense of humor, and I was recognizing and acknowledging the power of goodness within my spirit. These things were made much more attainable by the peace of mind I gleaned from the knowledge that the *body* part of the equation was being looked after by Dr.Schwartzentruber and all the other good and capable people at Goshen Hospital.

The side effects of the interleukin-2 were described to me beforehand like this: Imagine the worst case of the flu you have ever had, then, multiply that by a hundred. Ok, I could relate to that. I had dealt with the flu many times in my fifty-two years, just like everyone else. I didn't think of it at the time, but in my whole life I had been sick with a flu-like ailment maybe once a year. That would be fifty-two times at most, and I don't even think I was sick once a year as a kid. I was a pretty healthy little rug-rat. Now think of all the times in *your* life, dear reader, that you have been sick and then roll them all together into one week at whatever age you are now. You would be pretty doggone sick wouldn't you? Remember however, if you are in your fifties like me, you would still have to double *that* to have a hundred times the effect. If you are thirty-three, you would have to triple it. If you are twenty-five, you would have to *fourple* it! Now we begin to understand why I was in Intensive Care; this was supposed to be intense.

Still, I figured it was something I could handle. I mean shoot . . . what's a little fever, nausea, chills, achy joints, vomiting, and diarrhea, right? I fooled them though. I may have felt a hundred times nauseous, but I didn't throw up. I never have been much for that bit of nastiness. It has always taken a heck of a lot to make that happen. It's a good thing too, because the little yellow kidney-shaped plastic dish they give you to vomit into, only holds a few ounces, and it's so shallow, all it really provides is something off which to splash the putrid stuff.

Another side effect of the interleukin-2 therapy is a condition known as capillary leakage syndrome. This causes one to swell up like one of those giant balloons in the Macy's Thanksgiving Day parade. I'm exaggerating of course, but I did have the feeling throughout my therapy that if I wasn't careful, and if I wasn't attached to all those tubes and wires, I just might float up through the ceiling.

This swelling is caused by the leakage of fluids out of blood vessels into the surrounding tissue. This fluid can affect internal organs too. Dr. Schwartzentruber and the nurses all paid close attention to the sound of my lungs throughout the therapy. The capillary leakage can also cause a drop in blood pressure and a decrease in blood flow to body organs which can have its own side effects such as changes in the rhythm of the heartbeat, severe chest pains, difficulty breathing, heart attacks, decreased kidney functions, and decreased mental alertness. All of this is why one needs to be in generally good health before beginning the therapy. It's the reason for the heart stress test, and also why Dr. Schwartzentruber insisted that I be off cigarettes at least two weeks before beginning.

Incidentally, as serious as all the side effects of IL-2 can be, I would wager that the list of problems either caused or exacerbated by the tar and nicotine in tobacco would fill much more space than that required above.

I was just about to write that I think I'm getting ahead of myself, but seeing as how I believe that to be a physical impossibility, I think I am probably precisely where I should be, back in my ICU room with my brand new PICC line all hooked up and eagerly awaiting whatever comes next.

Eagerly awaiting? Yeah right! I don't mind telling you that no matter how I appeared to Kathy and Linda on the outside, on the inside I was thinking about all the things that could go wrong. Yes, I was having a bit of trouble keeping the old positive attitude going.

I had read all the literature. Dr. Schwartzentruber had answered every question I had thrown his way.

In the early clinical studies people had died from some of those IL-2 side effects of which I just spoke. Of course that was in the beginning, before they knew the capillary leakage thing was going to happen. They have that under control now. And what if I *didn't* have the therapy?

What if, while my curtain was pulled and nobody could see me, I quietly slipped out my second-floor window onto the roof? Then I could sneak across the roof to a fire escape . . . and do what? Escape, of course!

I would climb stealthily down the ladder, dexterously using just one hand on the rungs because the other would be holding the rear opening of my gown closed so as not to embarrass myself. Once on the ground, I would find an exterior maintenance door where, upon entering, I'm sure I could find a janitor's coverall which I would don to make myself less conspicuous. Ah, but I couldn't just *swipe* the custodial garment could I? No. I would be forever labeled a common thief by those who had originally sought nothing more than to be of help to me. No, I would have to discover where the grounds equipment was kept and use a garden tractor to mow the lawn as consideration for the clothing. That done, I could continue my carefully planned flight.

Kathy had left her cell phone in the minivan when we arrived. I could make my way to the vehicle and call my room. Kathy would, no doubt, answer and I would have her slip away unnoticed to meet me at the minivan where I would be cleverly concealed behind the rear seat. But no, I had no key to the van, and no change with which to use a payphone. I would have to leave Kathy a note on the windshield, held in place by a wiper blade; it worked for political flyers after all. I would then make my way behind the hospital. There is a river back there somewhere. Once at the water's edge, I'm sure I could find a log, or a large broken tree branch. I would use this to camouflage my actions, and as a floatation device to help get me downriver unseen until I could find the ideal location to make camp. Kathy would know from the note to watch for smoke from my fire, which I will have ignited using the lens of my eyeglasses. She would then find me and we would simply stay there and live happily ever after. UNTIL I DIED OF CANCER!

The metastatic melanoma - stage three (which is . . . you know) - would find me and snuff me out, most likely within the next eight months to a year! Besides, where was all that positive thinking I've been raving about, the power from within and all that? It's easy to revert to old ways when facing the unknown.

So I stayed in my hospital bed and Linda hooked me up to a contraption that monitored my heart rate, my blood pressure, the oxygen in my blood, how often I blinked my eyes, and when nobody was around, it dealt a mean two-handed game of Old Maid.

It was August 8, 2005, 4:00 pm, time for my first dose of interleukin-2. Linda administered it via my PICC line. She said it would take about fifteen minutes for the whole dose to enter my system. I was to receive a dose every eight hours until my body couldn't handle any more.

Kathy stood beside my bed, holding my hand. She kissed me on the cheek and smiled. I could see the worry in her eyes as I tried, in vain, to keep mine open. I slept.

Some time later, I opened my eyes and there was darkness at my window. The only light in the room came from the nurses' station, which was right outside my door, and the glow from the digital readouts on the monitors. All was still. The quiet was intense. You could have heard the proverbial pin drop, but I guess no one dropped one. The stillness was so radically different from all the hustle and bustle of that afternoon that I began to wonder if anyone was out there.

The whole wall of my room which faces the nurses' station was made of glass, including the extra-wide door, but the curtains could be drawn the entire length of the wall and that was the case now. I could see nothing except that which was within my room. I thought it must be the wee hours of the morning. I looked at the big, round, white-faced clock on the wall. Nine fifteen. That was all? As I looked away from the clock, pondering this, I caught an irregular movement from its face out of the corner of my eye. I looked back quickly, and nothing. Maybe it was a fly. I glanced around the room trying to locate the little bugger. But wait a minute here. This isn't Bangladesh. There shouldn't be flies in a hospital room, especially in the ICU! My eyes returned to the clock. I noticed something I hadn't before: The face really was a face. It looked like the "happy face" Wal-mart uses in its ads, only it was white instead of yellow, and of course it had hands angling off its dot of a nose. Did it have a face like that before? I didn't think so, but it must have. Why would anyone change wall clocks while I was sleeping? They wouldn't. That's absurd. I looked around for the fly again. I didn't want it to land on the end of the drinking straw that was sticking out of my water glass. Flies are nasty critters. They land on all sorts of foul, germ and bacteria-laden matter. Dead carcasses, poop, you name it. *Ah, that's where he is.* I thought.

He's hanging around the toilet on the other side of this curtain here! (In the ICU, the toilet is behind a curtain near the bed, not in its own separate room with a door.)

I could picture that fly just sitting there waiting and watching while he rubbed his front legs together in that anticipatory way that they do. I never heard any buzzing so he had to be just sitting there. The more I thought about it, the more I was convinced that not only was he indeed there, behind that curtain, he had now grown to the size of a football! My stomach gurgled. I realized with sudden terror that I needed to use that toilet behind there. But how could I? The fly was waiting. My stomach began to cramp. It was gurgling violently now. *Oh no, not the diarrhea they told me about!* I would have to make it to that toilet now. Flu symptoms, only a hundred times worse! *Lord help me. What can a hundred times the diarrhea be like?*

I realized I would not simply have to make it out of my bed to the other side of the curtain and take on the giant fly, I would have to do it while attached to all those tubes and wires and machines. What if I got out of bed only to find that I had no control, that I was maneuvered about by an unseen hand like a marionette? No. That was just silly. I had to get a grip. It was still too quiet outside my room. I thought of my nurse Linda. Maybe she would come to check on me soon and she could use a scalpel to skewer the deranged behemoth of a fly behind the curtain and flush him away. That's it, a nurse, any nurse. I couldn't afford to be too particular at the moment. Where was that darned call button? I found it clipped to my sheet and pressed it frantically several times. The TV came on and went off several times. What the heck is going on? I remembered not to cuss (Wasn't that what got me here in the first place?).

My stomach gurgled again, louder this time, more insistent. The nurse call button and the TV remote were on the same device. I had been hitting the power button for crying out Pete's sake! *There* was the button for the nurse, the *red* one. I glanced up at the clock. It was looking back at me, one eyebrow raised, a fly-food-eating grin on its face. I didn't remember it having eyebrows before. I looked away. My stomach was roiling now. I knew the mammoth fly must be rubbing his hands together gleefully, knowing that my time was about to run out (so to speak).

I pushed the red button and held it down. I was afraid to look back at the clock. I did anyway; I had to. It winked at me. Wait a minute! That's probably what I saw from the corner of my eye in the first place! It wasn't a fly. There had *never* been a fly! That's why I heard no buzzing. There was nothing frightening waiting behind the curtain after all, just a plain old hospital toilet. Boy did I feel foolish.

I managed to make my way out of bed and around the curtain, despite the tangle of lines that were hanging every which way. I was very weak and my joints hurt, but I did my business - which wasn't such an emergency as it turned out - and then after washing my hands at the little sink on the wall, I crawled back into bed between the cool sheets. I closed my eyes with a smile on my face, still feeling kind of foolish about how I had gotten myself all worked up over a nonexistent monster fly. *So silly!* I thought, snuggling the side of my face into the pillow and sighing. It was nothing more than the clock winking at me.

My eyes sprang open. I was lying on my side, the clock at my back. I knew if I turned around it would be staring at me, watching me, but I didn't think it would be smiling this time. In fact, I knew it

wouldn't. It would be glaring malevolently. The clock was angry. But

why? What had I done? I could feel its eyes on me, only I didn't

believe it was still on the wall. I thought I could sense it drawing

nearer. I could envision the face, twisted into an angry sneer. The

hands coming from its nose were actually little hands now, and the

clock was shaking its tiny fists at me. It wasn't just floating there in the

air behind me either. Oh no. It had the body of the killer fly and was

hovering above me on silent wings. It was rubbing those barbed legs

together as I was sure it had done before.

It was close now. If it had breath, I would have felt it upon my

neck. I wanted to scream for help, but nothing would come out of my

mouth. My throat was dry. I felt the sheet shift ever so slightly at my

back, and heard the soft rustle of the material as it did.

"Mr. Walton?" Now I screamed. "Mr. Walton, are you all

right?" It was a nurse, not Linda, but a nurse just the same. "I think

you might have been dreaming." She said. I turned over, not caring

much whether or not I disturbed the puppet strings. I looked at the clock. It was just a clock. No eyes, mouth, or eyebrows; just the hands with the arrows on the ends that it was supposed to have. It was nine-fifteen. There was the sound of activity outside my room. The curtains were open and I could see people out there. I looked at the nurse.

"The clock was watching me." I told her.

"The clock was watching you?" She repeated, looking puzzled.

"Yes, and there was a fly the size of a football." I said earnestly.

"A fly? In here?" She sounded skeptical.

"Behind the curtain." I insisted, pointing to the curtain hiding the toilet.

"I'm Betsy." The nurse said. She looked amused now. "I came on duty tonight at seven when Linda went off and I'll be taking care of you until seven tomorrow morning." She smiled knowingly then. "I think somebody forgot to tell you about the dreams, huh?"

"Yeah, I guess so." I said. "Wow."

During my stay in ICU that first week, I began to feel like I could handle anything. The nausea and the aches, and yes the diarrhea, all came calling, but I wasn't hit as hard as I had expected from all the warnings. The capillary leakage did cause me to swell up all over it's true. My fingers looked like so many fat sausages extending out from plump, fleshy paws. I put on twenty-four pounds of water in about three and a half days. My skin felt very tight, as if I were outgrowing it. I thought I must have looked a lot like the Michelin Man lying there in my bed.

My body handled ten doses of IL-2 that week. The tenth was on Thursday, August 11, 2005 at 4:00 pm. It seemed to me as if most of that week were spent inside a bubble that blurred everything around me. At least that's how it is in my memory. Sometime Friday Dr. Schwartzentruber ordered diuretics be given to me to help get rid of that extra water I just told you about.

Excuse me for saying so, but the first time I made my way to the bathroom after having been given the diuretic, I must have peed for about an hour and a half! I didn't know such a thing was possible. If only I'd had this trick at my disposal back when I was a kid! My female readers may not be aware of this, but little boys have peeing contests when no one is around, especially in the snow! They usually try to write their names in the snow before running out of steam (so to speak). Why, if I had had the diuretics available to me then, I would have been king!

When my weight had dropped to within five pounds of what it was when I was admitted, I was released from the hospital and Kathy took me home.

BE IT EVER SO HUMBLE

It was great to be back home. It was Sunday, August 14, 2005. All of my local family, who cared to, came to visit.

When I stepped out of the minivan Elvis began dancing around me like I was a giant rib-eye, and Ryan's smaller dog Kobe, was dancing around Elvis. I was a might woozy and wobbly on my feet so Kathy made sure I wasn't on them for long. The recliner in the living room, which actually belonged to Ryan, became my official comfort station. Elvis was so eager to be near me that he jumped right up into the chair with me and I was so weak I couldn't push him off. As you may recall, he is a hundred-pound dog. He was so comical that I

became even weaker with laughter and was helpless to stop him from

licking my face into oblivion.

Seeing my kids and grandkids was medicine itself - the best

kind. No matter how nauseous or achy I might have felt when first

arriving home, all of that was swept away by the love and concern I

saw in their eyes. Seeing my sisters Bea, and Brenda, and Brenda's

husband Jerry, touched my heart too. Then our son Sean and his girl

Eryn called from Virginia to complete the homecoming.

Of our other children, Andy, Autumn, and Rebecca, lived

within a few miles of us, and Ryan, as I've mentioned, still lived with

us. Andy and his wife Pilar have our grandson, Riley, who is seven,

and Becca and her husband, Sergio have our three granddaughters,

Charice, Alicia, and Alexis, who are ten, eight, and six respectively.

We have indeed been very blessed, not merely in having our five kids

and four grandkids, but also in the fact that they are all healthy and

fairly normal. Just *fairly* normal? You ask. Well, dear reader, you're

getting to know me by now, would you really expect any of my children to be *completely* normal?

THE MAGIC ELIXIR

During the two weeks I was home before returning to the
hospital for my second cycle of IL-2 therapy, a package arrived from
Kathy's sister Alex, who lives in Calgary, Alberta, Canada. The
package contained a box and inside the box were four bottles. The
bottles each held a little less than a quart of a liquid that was a deep
purplish-red in color. It was the juice of a fruit of which I had never
heard: The mangosteen fruit. According to the literature that Alex sent
with the juice, the mangosteen (no relation to the mango), has been
used as a folk remedy in Asia for centuries and is now attracting the
attention of scientists and physicians here and in Europe. It's about the
size of a tangerine and has a smooth purple surface with four to eight
white, oblong segments inside. Reportedly, the natives of Southeast
Asia use the mangosteen as an antioxidant, an anti-bacterial, and an
anti-inflammatory. What caught *my* eye in the literature was the part
that said the fruit contains Garcinone E, an anti-tumor agent. Those

words virtually jumped off the page at me.

See what I mean about the positive influences I was receiving? I was literally drawing positive energy from all directions. Alex had a career going up there in Calgary, a life of her own with all its demands and challenges. She could have simply said to herself, "Gee, I hope Chuck does alright with that cancer thing of his down there in the States. It sure would be a bummer for Kathy if he kicked off." But she didn't. She actively got involved and did what she could from afar. That mangosteen juice is kind of pricey too!

Now, I am not saying that the juice is responsible for my recovery (I know you didn't just fall off a turnip truck). I don't know what it did for me physically, but I do know this: I began taking the recommended dosage right away after reading the literature and it was one more thing that caused me to look forward. It was positive input. As I said before, anything and everything, right? When I refer to the mangosteen juice as a "magic elixir", I am sincere in that I believe there is magic in the genuine caring and concern that Alex exhibited by sending it to me. That's the kind of thing that touches your heart, and your heart touches your soul, and that is our link to the *real* magic. It's like the blessings from the nuns, the prayers from my family, both here and in Canada, the visit with Monika, the gifts of the two books, the chance discovery of Dr. Schwartzentruber and all the good people at Goshen Center For Cancer Care and hospital, the visits and phone calls from my kids, the adoring look in the soft brown eyes of a big black dog, and the devotion and love of my soul-mate Kathy. These are all things that I felt touch my soul and which helped me to tap in to the magic of the power of all that is good.

ELVIS HAS LEFT THE BUILDING

Speaking of our "big black dog" above reminded me of what I have to tell you next.

As I've mentioned, our business was crashing and burning around our ears. Not only was the cost of diesel fuel skyrocketing during this period, we lost drivers, trucks were in and out of the shop, *I* was in and out of the shop. Medical bills were piled up so high that we didn't think we'd ever see the sun again. In all of this mess the worst loss that we had to face was the loss of our big, beautiful black labrador retriever, Elvis.

We were no longer going to have our home with the huge fenced-in yard where Elvis had been able to run and play with very few restrictions all of his four-year-old life. The "For Sale" signs were up and we would soon be moving to a small house in town with a very tiny yard. We agonized over what to do about Elvis because we knew that he had such a free spirit that he would be miserable if the only time he was allowed outside was at the end of a leash.

The words "almost always fatal" had made an impression on me as far as my thinking about Kathy's future was concerned. I had to face the fact that it was possible that she would be alone in the months to come and she would no longer be working from home every day.

One day Elvis and I were sitting out by the pool in our back yard where he had just taken a dip. (Elvis even had his own set of pool stairs so he could go swimming any time he wanted and be able to walk right out on his own. We purchased those steps especially for him because, although he could climb the ladder, he wasn't very good at it and we didn't want to have to worry when we were away. Was he spoiled? Maybe a little.) The phone rang. It was someone who had heard about our predicament with Elvis, someone we had known for a long time and thought we could trust. As it turned out, she and her husband had recently lost their dog to illness and missed him terribly. I'll give you three guesses as to what type of dog they had. That's right, a Lab, a chocolate Lab! Did they have a huge fenced-in yard? You know they did! It seemed, at the time, like another prayer answered.

A couple of days after the phone conversation, Elvis went to live with them. When he was picked up, he jumped right in the back seat of the car as soon as the door was opened. He just sat there looking out at us with a big grin on his face, his soft brown eyes filled with excitement. I could imagine him saying, "C'mon! C'mon! Let's go! Where we goin? You comin Chuck? You comin Kathy? Let's-go-let's-go-let's-go!"

Kathy and I sent along Elvis's toys and other personal things, including his medical records, then stood in the road, arms around each other, and watched them drive away. Elvis stuck his head out the window and looked back at us, but he was clearly too excited about "going for a ride" to worry that we weren't coming along. That had *never* happened before.

"Bye Elvis." I heard Kathy whisper. Tears were streaming down her cheeks.

"Goodbye you big ol' goofball." I said quietly. We held each other close in our sadness, as what had just occurred really began to sink in.

You may be thinking that we could visit Elvis and we thought about that. We decided we couldn't. Not only would it bring back the sadness anew, it would be unfair to Elvis. After acclimating to his new life it would be very confusing for him to see us again, along with all the old familiar scents. Besides, I couldn't guarantee that I wouldn't selfishly demand to have him back once I saw him again. He was my buddy. As it turned out, I wish I had.

A few months after giving Elvis up I was driving in the general vicinity of our old house (we had since moved to the little house in

town that I mentioned before) and decided, on the spur of the moment,
to drive down our old road on the way home. I had no particular reason
for doing this. As a matter of fact, Kathy and I usually avoided taking
this road because of the feeling of loss it induced. Before I knew it
however, I had passed the old place and was pulling off to the side of
the road next to the big field where I used to sometimes take Elvis for
training exercises and to play ball. I just sat there thinking about all
that had occurred. I glanced into the rear-view mirror and imagined
that I saw him! He was running toward me down the road, ears
flapping, tongue lolling, and he was grinning like he always did
whenever he managed to get outside our big fenced yard untethered.
That grin and the impish gleam in his eyes said to the world, "I'm free!
I know I'm faster than you, and I'm going exploring!" Of course this
image faded and blinked out as I realized Elvis couldn't be physically
there, but it seemed so real for that brief moment. I told Kathy about it
and then the following night I had the dream:

I woke in the middle of the night and Elvis was standing at the
side of the bed with his head on my pillow as he had countless times in

the past. It's a king-size pillow and *my* head was on it too, so his snout was almost touching my nose. He was watching my face and when I opened my eyes his tail began wagging his body excitedly and he gave me a big ol' sloppy kiss on my eye. He was happy to see me, and I him. I can't describe aptly to you just how good it was to see him. I took his big head in both my hands and roughed up his ears affectionately, all the while telling him how glad I was that he was back. At some point I fell back to sleep and when I woke up the next morning he was gone.

That is the day I wrote in this book about having to give him up and watching him ride away. The day after that I got a call from the people he had gone to live with. They'd had Elvis put to sleep!

That's one way of saying it. The other is that they had him killed! And why? Did he have some terminal illness that would be excruciatingly painful for him to bear another moment? No, he did not! He had developed a growth on the tip of his tail, which had to be removed, and then his tail had to be stitched up. He then broke it open again by whacking it on things while wagging it. He was *always* wagging his tail - what a terrible dog! The woman told me that her vet said Elvis's tail would have to be removed and she had decided to have him "put to sleep" because it was going to cost too much MONEY! It wasn't life threatening at all. It was just going to COST TOO MUCH! And get this: This had all taken place TWO months before! She called me on July 14, and this had taken place on Memorial Day weekend!

I sat there staring at the phone in shock, but I managed to control my voice enough to ask this woman, whom I thought was giving our beloved friend a good, happy, and SAFE home, if she had read Elvis's medical file that we had sent along with him. She said she had. In that case, she must have seen that Kathy and I had spent a whole bunch of money and lots of time nursing Elvis back to health when he was a puppy and had apparently eaten a poisonous toadstool or something.

I was on the road when it happened but Kathy was with him every night. By day he was with Dr. Bob and Dee at Three Point Veterinary Clinic in Elkhart, Indiana hooked up to an I.V. At closing time Kathy picked him up and cared for him at home every minute. He finally came out of it and grew into the big solid lug that we loved. Dr. Bob referred to Elvis as his "miracle dog".

Now he's dead, and I only gave him up because I thought *I* was going to be dead and I didn't want Kathy to have to make all the tough decisions alone. This person that I was foolish enough to give Elvis to didn't even call and give us the option to take Elvis back and care for him ourselves. Remember, she didn't call *at all* for two months!

I asked her what happened to his body. She said he was cremated. Ok, what was done with his ashes? She didn't know. Apparently, once she had made the decision that Elvis was more trouble than he was worth, she had just washed her hands of the whole thing.

I still had to give Kathy this news. When I did, she was absolutely devastated. This was just beyond her comprehension. Of course it was. It was something she would never, ever, even *think* about doing.

I know animal lovers understand exactly how we feel about this whole thing. People who aren't animal lovers may think the words I've just written concerning the loss of our dog to be silly and bitter. They're bitter all right. I'll give you that. But geez, Elvis was our buddy. He was *not* supposed to die.

I tried to think about all I had learned throughout my ordeal with the cancer up to that point. Where was the positive in this? They say that to forgive is divine. Well I wasn't feeling all that divine just then and as far as I was concerned, God could forgive them. I didn't necessarily have to.

Originally in this book I had named the people who had Elvis killed. I went back and changed all that. That's *something* isn't it?

I suppose you could say that the image I had of Elvis running free, and the dream where he came to see me in the night were positive things, indications that his soul is now free, and that he is happy. As a matter of fact, one could wonder why those things occurred just before I received the news of his "passing" if they were *not* positive signs. There may be some out there right now reading this who are thinking to themselves that animals don't have souls. To Kathy and me that is utter nonsense. We have only to envision those warm brown eyes and remember the love, the loyalty, the innocence, and the joy of living that was there, to know that Elvis was, and is, a pure soul. And that's all I have to say about that.

IMAGINE THAT

On August 29, 2005 I returned to the ICU at Goshen Hospital for my second cycle of IL-2 therapy. Like before, I was wheeled down to have my PICC line inserted and then brought back to my room and hooked up to all the gadgets. My first dose this time around, like the first, was to be at 4:00 pm, and I think it was about 3:00 when Dr. Schwartzentruber came in to see me.

"How's it going?" He asked, smiling warmly.

"Not bad. My hands and feet have pretty much healed up now." I replied, shaking his offered hand.

I forgot to mention that the first week of IL-2 had caused my hands and feet to crack, and the skin peeled away in layers. My hands had been bright red and raw, and the soles of my feet had peeled off in such big, thick slabs that I joked with Kathy that I could probably make her a pair of moccasins out of them if she might fancy a pair. She declined.

"That's good." Said Dr. Schwartzentruber. "Now let's have a look at those nodules." He had already told me that we shouldn't expect much change in them until after I had been through the second cycle of doses. That would complete one "course" of therapy, and then I would have four to six weeks off. After the time off we would decide if the IL-2 was doing any good and if a second course (two cycles) was warranted.

I was watching his face as he pulled aside the sheet and a portion of the gown that covered my leg. I, of course, already knew what he was going to see. I noted the look of surprise.

"We already have a response." He said, looking up at me. I was grinning.

"I know." I said. "It's not supposed to happen that fast, is it?"

"I don't recall ever having this type of response this soon." He poked and prodded. "If I'm not mistaken, some of the smallest nodules have all but faded away completely."

"Yes, they have." I said.

"These larger ones show definite signs of shrinking too." He said.

"Those were the first to appear, so they've had more time to grow." I replied.

"Hold on. Kristan's just outside the room somewhere. I want her to see this." Kristan Reinheimer is one of two Nurse Practitioners who work closely with Dr. Schwartzentruber. The other is Deena Gonyon. I met them both my first week. They are both very professional and caring women. Dr. Schwartzentruber returned with Kristan in tow. He uncovered my leg again.

"You see?" He said. "Do you remember what they looked like before?"

"Yes, of course." Said Kristan. This is fantastic."

"This is very exciting." Dr. Schwartzentruber agreed.

Imagine that. That's all I can do, only imagine what it must be like for Dr. Schwartzentruber to see such promising results as he did that day with me. To put it into perspective, he worked all of those many years helping to develop this new therapy and he knows the statistics concerning its effectiveness better that anyone. He knows that metastatic melanoma kills. He knows that, in me, it has already traveled to thirty different locations from the original tumor. He knows that once it gets to a person's organs, the mean time that person has left to live is approximately six to eight months. He also knows that the IL-2 therapy is effective in only about sixteen percent of people, and a real reversal only occurs in about six percent.

So after all the years and with all that knowledge, it must have indeed been exciting to see, in my case, such positive results after just the first week of doses. I know it was for me! Just seeing and hearing his reaction was such a positive boost for me that I'm surprised the remaining melanoma nodules on my leg didn't just drop off onto the floor right then and there!

ROUND TWO

"Whoa! What's going on here?" That's what I heard myself saying to Kathy after the first of my second-cycle doses. This wasn't like the first time. It hit me fast and hard. Dr. Schwartzentruber came back in to see me and told me that this was normal.

Apparently, when my body received the first round of IL-2 it didn't know, immediately, what to do with it. Then of course it figured things out and sent the doses where they were needed. This second time around there was no such delay. My body *remembered* where to send the interleukin-2 and BAM! It sent it directly where it was meant to be. It didn't pass "GO", and it definitely didn't collect two hundred dollars (Kathy would have told me).

I was sick, and weak, and although my diet was unrestricted, I didn't feel like eating much. I wondered how many doses my body could take this time. All I wanted to do was sleep so that I could get through this and feel it as little as possible. Sleep, if I could only sleep . . .

I looked around me. Kathy was gone. She had just been standing there holding my hand and talking quietly to me. She was telling me how, before I knew it, I would be out of here and back at home where she would take care of me. That was comforting. I remember smiling up at her. Had I closed my eyes? I must have. But I don't remember doing it. No, I think I just looked away momentarily and when I looked back she was gone.

Could she have just vanished into thin air? Now that I thought about it, nobody could. Thin air won't hide anything. It would have to be *thick* air, *very* thick air! It would have to be so thick that it could be folded over on top of something, or someone, to conceal them. Ok, but if the air was that thick, how could I breathe it? I couldn't. I began to gasp. I couldn't get my breath! It was like trying to inhale some ghostly molasses! I was suffocating right here in the Intensive Care Unit! I looked frantically for the nurse call button. It was clipped to my sheet somewhere but I couldn't see it. The sheet was too wavy. No, it was the air. The *air* was too wavy! The rolling swells of air came together in front of my face and were tucked into my open mouth the way a curtain can accidentally get caught up in a vacuum cleaner. I was clutching at them madly with both hands, but there was nothing substantial to get hold of. Thick or not, it was still air and I could feel it slipping frustratingly through my fingers like a heavy breeze. Suddenly

I noticed movement from the corner of my eye. My head jerked automatically in that direction. It had to be a nurse, but it wasn't. It was a door. I knew I was on the verge of blacking out as the door began to ease open. It opened only a crack, maybe three inches at most, but that was enough.

The curtain of air that was clogging my mouth and throat at once withdrew itself and, joining the rest of the crazily undulating mass in the center of the room, began to swirl into a cyclonic funnel that was instantly sucked horizontally through the door and out of my room. Then the door clicked softly shut. I lay there gasping and watching the door until my breathing returned to normal.

It was a door that hadn't been there before. The wall had been there all right, but not the door. It was an ordinary enough looking door. It looked like one of the interior doors from my old house as a matter of fact. It was a six-panel wooden door about six and a half feet high and about two and a half feet wide with a shiny brass handle. The door was still closed and didn't appear ominous in any way. For that matter, hadn't it just saved my life? If anything, the door radiated a calmness, a sturdy tranquility that put me at ease.

The door remained closed but I somehow knew that it would open again if I climbed out of bed and approached it. I knew that no matter how sick and weak I felt at the moment, getting up and crossing the room to that door would be effortless. I knew that I wouldn't even need to be concerned about the tangle of tubes and wires that had become my constant hindrances because if my intention was to pass through that doorway, they would all just melt away, simply cease to be there.

I was awed by this door but was not compelled to use it. It was as if it had been made available to me, and nothing more. I remember smiling at the door with a newfound awareness, and feeling myself drift off to sleep unafraid. When I awoke, I told others about the door, but this came from the very same guy who had shared with them the terror of the dreadful clock-faced fly.

That week my body took in six doses of interleukin-2 before it communicated to Dr. Schwartzentruber that it had had enough.

By the way, I know you've probably already figured this out, oh wise reader, but Kathy never really vanished that day.

HANGIN IN THERE

After the second cycle it was five weeks before I had new scans and blood work and returned to see Dr. Schwartzentruber for a follow up. Everything still looked good. The tumors were continuing to retreat, and still at a faster rate than usual. Dr. Schwartzentruber and company were still excited about the speed at which my body seemed to be fighting off the cancer with the aid of the interleukin-2 therapy. I was too of course, although I wasn't out of the woods yet and Dr. Schwartzentruber scheduled me for a second course, which would mean two more weeks (cycles) of doses. I wasn't looking forward to that, but I knew it had to be done. The IL-2 was working and we were all very optimistic. It's just that every dose had become harder and harder to take. Knowing that I was going back for more, on purpose, became something to dread as the time drew nearer.

The time *did* arrive, as it always does, and on October 17, 2005, again on a Monday, I found myself back in the I.C.U. at Goshen hospital.

Kathy was with me as always. I checked in and went through the PICC line rigmarole and all the rest of the preparation. Dr. Schwartzentruber came in to see me in the afternoon to make sure all systems were "go", and then at 4:00 pm I received my first dose of this new "course", my seventeenth in all. My diet was unrestricted as usual, but as soon as the dose hit I knew I wouldn't be eating much of anything this time around. I was immediately nauseous, although I didn't actually throw up. I just retained the feeling that I was about to, almost as bad, but not quite.

I was a lousy visit once the IL-2 therapy had begun. I knew it too. I had told friends and family that they didn't need to disrupt their days by traveling the forty minutes to Goshen (each way) to visit someone who wasn't much fun to be around. Kathy was there every day though. Sometimes I would suddenly realize there was someone in my room, and it would be Kathy and Rebecca, or Kathy and Ryan, or Autumn would come on her own. Either Kathy or Autumn brought me a chocolate malted milk-shake almost every day. It was the one thing I knew I could get down and actually enjoy. I don't know if they realized how much I looked forward to seeing them appear with that big white Steak n Shake cup in their hands.

My father's brother, Jerry, and his wife Rose, came to see me one day. They live in Connecticut and were in town for a reunion of some kind. I distinctly remember them sitting across the room from me, and I believe we had a long and pleasant visit, but I can't seem to recall anything we talked about. I *do* remember thinking it was great seeing them after so many years. I hadn't seen them since my Grandma Walton's funeral. She was Jerry's (and my dad's) mother. That was a very sad day for all of us because Grandma Walton was one of those people who was immediately loved by everyone with whom she made contact. She had always been there in my life. Her little brick house was a sanctuary for both my sister Brenda and me after our mother remarried. It was the only place we ever saw a picture of our dad. No such thing was allowed in our stepfather's house (which was built by our father and grandfather), but there was always an 8x10 photo of our dad prominently on display in our grandparent's living room. There was an even larger picture of him on that wall that our grandfather had painted.

Although I still miss my grandmother's physical presence in my life, I now understand that she is still with me and always will be, as you shall see a little later on.

I was very sick when I returned home from the hospital this time around, but gradually as the days passed I grew stronger. I was getting stronger so I could go back and do it all over again. I meditated at night when Kathy was asleep. I was still having trouble sleeping myself unless I took myself to that peaceful place. I wondered at times if I would be able to sustain the kind of strength I was going to need to complete the IL-2 therapy. It really kicked my butt this second time around. I had recently seen an example of real strength and character however, and I kept it in mind as the days and treatments progressed.

BRENDA

I can't possibly imagine the depths of emotion into which a woman is plunged when she hears from her doctor that she has breast cancer. That's the news my sister Brenda received one day not long after I had the two surgeries on my leg. She and I have always been close, but for the two of us to be dealing with cancer at the same time, is a little more "in tune" than we need to be.

I remember when she told me that a lump had been discovered during her latest mammogram, something she hadn't had done in about ten years. Brenda is slightly more than a year older than I, and she was pretty upset with herself for not having regular mammograms as her doctor had advised. The lump turned out to be malignant.

Surgery was scheduled and the lump was removed. We all believed the crisis to be over and then the cancer returned. Brenda has since had a double mastectomy and appears now to be cancer-free, but what a cost!

I learned from my sister during that troubled period. I learned that she was very afraid, but realized she didn't want to be *seen* as afraid. She doesn't like to "burden" others with her problems. Brenda has always been internally strong like that, something she learned from our grandmother no doubt. It was an amazing thing, the way she handled the loss of both breasts. She said she was "getting tired of carrying those things around anyway". In Brenda's case, what she gave up was substantial too, if you know what I mean. I remember that it was always difficult to squeeze through a doorway at the same time she was sidling through. I used to joke with her that she hadn't just been blessed physically; she had been endowed with "real estate".

Though Brenda could joke about her loss outwardly, I know that on the inside it was all extremely painful to her. I've been her brother forever and I could see it in her eyes. She had the support of her family of course, her kids, her husband Jerry's parents, Kathy, my sister Bea, and I. But the person who gave her the most confidence and help in accepting what had to be was, and is, her husband Jerry. When the whole ordeal began he told her that no matter what, he loves her for who she is, not for how she looks, and he meant it. It shows every time I see them. Jerry has true character to match Brenda's and I've thanked God many more times than he might believe for bringing him into my sister's life.

I was positive for Brenda when she told me the cancer had

returned because I knew she would be for me. I couldn't let on just how hard that news had hit me. In fact I refused to believe that the outcome could be anything *but* positive. Brenda has always been a part of my life. Since she is older, there has never been a time when she wasn't there. She has always been more than my sister. She has been my friend and confidant. It just wasn't conceivable to me that she could *not* be there.

Brenda's positive attitude rubbed off on the rest of us and I'm sure had a lot to do with her eventual positive prognosis. When later I found out that my own cancer had returned, I tried to follow her example and open myself to any affirming influences I could find.

I remember telling Brenda one day that if I was supposed to go first, it was ok because I would be able to check everything out and get to know my way around so that when the rest of them came to join me, they wouldn't have any fears or apprehensions. It would be great when we were all back together! I meant that too. It was a very positive feeling thinking that I could help all the people I love make their final transition, and perhaps provide them with peace of mind in *their* last hours because they would know that I was there waiting for them.

Perhaps you, dear reader, are experiencing a particularly challenging time in your life, or know someone who is. Seek out the positive all around you. You will find strength and hope where you had despair, and faith will fill your heart.

Faith in what? I've already told you that I don't consider myself to be a particularly religious individual and that hasn't changed as far as organized religion goes. But my spiritual beliefs, now that's a different story. I *do* have faith my friend. I have faith that goodness wins. I have faith that goodness is God. I have faith that love is the essence of goodness and therefore of God. I have faith that from this pure love our souls have their beginnings, and our souls are who we really are. I have faith that our souls are our source of healing power over our bodies. And above all else, I have faith that when our human experiences have come to an end, whether that be sooner or later, and we return to our pure forms, our souls, we will realize that there had never been any reason to fear anything, ever, and we will thank God for our experience in humanity for without it, how could we have appreciated the difference?

GRANDMA

One of the nights during my fourth week of interleukin-2, I had a rather unsettling experience. I know what you're thinking: *He's going to tell me about another one of his weird dreams.* Well, I suppose it *was* a dream, although at the time I didn't think I was asleep. I guess you'll have to decide for yourself.

Kathy had just left my room to return home for the evening, and I was lying in my bed observing, through a thin veil of fog, the activity outside my room. The people out there were speaking normally, but they were all moving in slow motion. Suddenly I realized my nurse, Sharon, was standing by my bed. I didn't see her come in and I would have sworn she wasn't already in the room when Kathy left. She was looking at her watch while taking my pulse.

"Whoa! Where'd *you* come from?" I asked, startled.

"You mean originally?" She asked.

"No. Just now." I said. "You weren't standing there a second ago."

"Shh." She said. "I'm taking your pulse."

"What are you going to do with it?" I asked.

"With what?"

"My pulse. You can't just *take* it. I'm pretty sure I'm gonna need it. In fact, I think I use it a lot. No, you can't have it." I pulled my arm away and hid it under the sheet. Sharon put her hands on her hips.

"I didn't want to do this, but you leave me no choice." She said as she rolled the foot of my bed toward the door. She then came around to the head and began pushing the whole bed toward the door.

"Where are we going?" I asked, alarmed. I looked up and she was looking down at me as she continued to push. All her features were upside-down. I remembered all the wires and tubes I was attached to and glanced worriedly in that direction. They weren't coming with us. They were all breaking off, one by one! As each tube or wire was stretched beyond its limit and snapped, it issued a loud twang like a tortured ukulele string. What was happening here?

"Sharon stop, they're all breaking!" I cried. I forced my eyes back up in her direction, afraid of what I might see. She wasn't there! I looked around frantically. She was nowhere to be seen, but the bed was still moving! I tried to roll out of it but I couldn't raise my body. The sheets were holding me down as if they were tucked snugly, with great force, under all the edges of the mattress, but they weren't. They appeared to be just lying there loosely.

The bed was taking me through the door now. I was out in the hallway. There was Sharon, talking to another nurse. Both of them seemed to be oblivious of me. How could they not see me? I suddenly realized that Sharon couldn't have been in my room with me just moments ago. So who was?

"Sharon!" I screamed. She didn't hear me! I was still traveling down the hall, getting farther and farther away. Sharon and the other nurse became tiny figures at the other end of the tunnel, well over a hundred yards away. *Tunnel?* This was a hallway in the hospital! No, it *was* a tunnel and, just as I realized this to be the case, the lights went out. It was black as pitch, no light whatsoever.

I struggled against the sheet. I had one free hand, my right hand. I had hidden my left hand under the sheet to keep the faux Sharon from stealing my pulse and now it was trapped there, useless to me. I couldn't sit up. I couldn't roll over. I extended my free arm and felt all around me in the darkness. Nothing.

What was that? I thought I had heard something, something very faint and far away. There it was again! I knew that sound. It was the sound of a car speeding down an asphalt road, and it was getting closer. I raised my head and looked toward the sound. I could just barely make out the outline of my toes under the sheet. There was dim light now, but it was brightening as the roar of that rocketing engine drew nearer. Now I could clearly see two round white lights growing larger and brighter by the second. The car was coming too fast. Would the driver see me? Would he see me in time? The sweat that had been beading on my forehead now began to roll down into my eyes. I felt a random drop run into my ear. I began shouting hysterically and waving my free arm in the air.

"STOP! STOP! I'M HERE! SEE ME? I'M HERE! STOP!"

There was no change in the sound of the engine as it screamed down on my location. The lights were almost blinding now. I was dead! I came to this hospital to try to keep cancer from killing me, and now here I was, about to be crushed and ripped to shreds hideously by some maniacal speeding car while I was strapped helplessly in my hospital bed, which was sitting in the middle of the hospital hallway!

"FINE THEN!" I screamed, as I glared back at those headlights. "HERE I AM! COME ON!"

All at once there was the long high-pitched screeching of tires on asphalt and I could see the car sliding sideways toward me. It came to a stop after bumping my bed ever so slightly. Dense smoke was thick in the headlight beams and the smell of burned rubber was almost overpowering.

I found myself staring at the side of a black 1960 Chevy Impala. It glistened in the night. I could see myself faintly in the sheen of the door. I realized I was holding my breath and began to breathe again, tasting the microscopic tire particles in the air. Someone was getting out of the opposite side of the car, the driver's side. He walked around

the front of the car and I watched him pass through the headlights,
though the smoke was so thick I couldn't make him out clearly. There
was something familiar about his walk. He approached my bed and
was almost in full view when he said,

"Can't you get up?" I recognized the voice immediately. It was
Rick. My friend Rick had died in an auto accident when we were in
our late twenties. We had been friends since we were about seven
years old after having met in the second grade. We had spent many
nights in our teens cruising country roads and listening to old-time rock
n roll on WLS AM out of Chicago. Rick always had the wheels.

"No. If I could, I would." I said. He grabbed hold of the sheet
and whipped it back and off me, and I was free! Just like that. It now
seemed perfectly normal for him to be there and he didn't seem to think
it was odd that I hadn't been able to get out from under the sheet on my
own.

"Let's get out of here." He said. It occurred to me that I would
be cruising in my hospital gown, but when I looked down I realized it
had vanished, as apparently had the bed. I was wearing jeans and a

black Harley Davidson T-shirt. Scuffed motorcycle boots were on my feet. I recognized them. I had owned them when I was seventeen. I felt great. I felt young!

We both hopped into the car, Rick dropped the transmission into first gear, and we roared away, burning another layer of rubber off the Chevy's tires. Rick cranked up the volume on the eight-track and the rolling drum beat of *Radar Love* filled the night. He looked over at me and grinned, and that's when I remembered: We had done this once before.

When I originally heard about Rick's fatal accident I was on the road traveling in a big truck (other people call them "semis", truckers call them "big trucks"). I arranged for a trip home so that I could go to the funeral home and pay my respects to Rick's family. There was no way I could *not* be there.

On the way home, in a rest area, while sleeping in the bunk, I dreamed that I was standing along a dark highway and Rick stopped to pick me up. As we were cruising along, I realized that I had just been in the process of heading home to Rick's funeral. I also instantly awakened to the fact that wherever he was going, *I* was definitely *not* going, at least not just yet, and I told him so. He had shrugged off what I had said and declared, "The night has just started!" I told him again that I couldn't go with him and insisted, demanded, that he pull over and let me out, which he did, grudgingly. Then he roared away into the night and I woke up shivering. I have always wondered, if I had stayed in that car, would I have ever again awakened to this life?

Now it was happening all over again, and I realized it again.

"Rick. RICK!" I reached over and turned the music down. "Rick, listen to me."

"Aw, that was a good song man!"

"Yeah, yeah I know." I said. "Rick, do you remember the last time we went for a ride like this?"

"Yeah I remember." He said with a grin.

"Well, I couldn't go where you were going then, and I can't go where you're going now."

"Sure you can man!"

"No, I can't. You're going to have to pull over and let me out this time too."

"How do you know you can't go?" He asked.

"The same as last time." I said. I didn't want to come right out and say the words. I didn't know what would happen if I had to remind him that he wasn't exactly alive anymore.

"But it's *not* the same as last time." He said, knowingly.

"What do you mean?" I said. "Sure it is." But I thought I was beginning to understand.

"*You* are not the same." He replied matter-of-factly. "You're way more than halfway there already. So what's better, cruisin' with your best friend, or seeing what's behind Door Number One?" A chill swept through me. Was he talking about "the" door? Somehow I knew he was.

"How do you know about the door Rick?"

"How do you think? I didn't have a best friend to pick *me* up and go cruisin'."

"No, I guess you didn't." I half whispered. "But you still need to pull over and let me out. I'm not going right now."

"C'mon man. Really, you're closer than you think already."

"Pull over Rick."

"But listen man . . ."

"Now, Rick."

"Aw man!" He pulled the Impala over onto the shoulder. "You used to be a *lot* more fun." He pointed out.

"I'll be fun again." I said. "But later, *much* later I hope." I tried to open the door. It wouldn't budge. I looked at Rick. He was smiling sheepishly. "Unlock the door." I said. He spread his hands, palms up, and shrugged.

" I didn't lock 'em." He said. This car doesn't have power locks." But there was mischief in his eyes.

Suddenly headlights came on out of the blackness beside us and glared full force into the Chevy. I just about jumped out of my skin, which, if you think about it, is exactly what my friend Rick wanted me to do. I squinted toward the lights. I could just make out the chrome strip around the grill of a sixty-four Studebaker Lark just like the one my Grandma Walton used to have. Grandma?

"Ricky, you stop that tom-foolery this instant and let him get that door open!" That was Grandma's voice all right, I'd know it anywhere. She'd known Rick a long time too. His dad used to deliver home heating oil to her house way back when.

I heard a click from the door and tried it again. It opened and I climbed out. I just barely got myself clear before Rick peeled out and, in a flash, was nothing but taillights, and then those winked out. I turned and faced the brilliant white light that radiating from Grandma's old Studebaker. The car was white its self and glittered and gleamed in the blinding light. I shielded my eyes and tried to see my grandmother behind the wheel. I knew somehow that I couldn't get into the Lark with her.

"How do I get back?" I called. "Grandma, which way is back? I don't even know where I am!"

"Due north." She answered softly, and I could hear her as well as if she were just inches from my ear. "It's just dawdling to go sideways, and you never, ever, want to go south! Due north, always due north." And with that the light became so bright that I couldn't see any part of the old Studebaker anymore.

"But I don't even know where I am!" I cried desperately.

"Due north." I heard her say again, very faintly this time. "Just remember . . ." Her voice faded completely away.

"What?" I said again. The light was much less intense now so I blinked open my eyes. There was a young nurse leaning over me. Her nametag read Debbie, or Deb. I tried to focus.

"Two North Mr. Walton." She was saying. "You're on Two North, in recovery." They always brought me to the north side of the second floor when I was in the recovery faze of the interleukin-2 therapy.

"Oh." I said. "Oh yeah, I remember."

Now, I know that the interleukin-2 can produce some pretty bizarre dreams, but lying there thinking about that one, I couldn't help but wonder just how close I had really come to completing that drive with Rick this time while I was sleeping. It wasn't really a frightening thing. It was more like it just felt wrong, like I was being rushed and I wasn't supposed to be. Grandma Walton seemed to know it too and that's why she stepped in.

WEEK FIVE OF IL-2 (THE LAST ONE)

After the fourth week of the interleukin-2 therapy, and after having waited the usual six weeks or so for my scans and blood work, I had my check-up with Dr. Schwartzentruber and the melanoma seemed to be completely gone.

That was wonderful news and I thought I would be finished with the therapy, but Dr. Schwartzentruber suggested that I have one more cycle - another week's worth - for good measure.

Most who have undergone the therapy before me have had to endure it for at least *seven* weeks so I was thankful that I would be stopping at five. I felt so drained already, like somebody had actually pulled my plug and all my "juice" was running out.

Remember, each week I spent in Intensive Care was a week in which my body was in what I heard referred to as a "controlled crash". My blood pressure often dropped into the seventies-over-fifties range, my heart rate would frequently shoot up to 140 or so, I had the nasty poops whether I was eating or not, I felt like I was always, at any second, going to throw up so violently that my whole mattress would be sucked up my butt and come flying out of my mouth, and of course the capillary leakage thing caused me to swell up so that lying there in my bed, I very closely resembled a big fat walrus stranded on a rock outcropping out in the middle of somewhere. So, knowing that I was going to have to return for one more cycle, when I thought I was finished, made me groan just ever so slightly (inside, I was whining like a little girl).

On December 12, 2005, when week five actually began, it was comforting to know that it really would be the last cycle. This time though, the IL-2 hit me hardest as you might expect. I didn't even want to *smell* any food. Even the malted milk shakes that Autumn & Kathy continued to bring me faithfully, weren't appealing the way they had been previously.

I was just kind of floating along in a cloud, a cloud that seemed to have worked its way into my mind because that week is even fuzzier than the others when I think back on it. I do know that I again wanted to just sleep through the whole week if that were possible, but of course

it wasn't (too many trips to the commode on the other side of the

curtain, if you know what I mean).

Somehow this time around, I did manage to make it to the last

dose of interleukin-2 (the sixth this cycle). I remember my nurse,

Twilight, talking to me (yes, her name is really Twilight) and I watched

her just sort of fade out as I drifted off to sleep. I remember feeling

very peaceful at that moment, like there was nothing at all in the world

that would disturb me or give me cause for concern. Then I was

suddenly elated and feeling a very simple and basic happiness . . .

"Throw it high Daddy! Throw it way high!" I was six years

old and playing catch with my dad in the back yard at our little house

on Jane street. I was thoroughly impressed with my dad's ability to

seemingly throw a baseball clear up into the clouds so that it virtually

disappeared before hurtling down toward where I was standing with my

little glove, hoping to catch it and hear my dad's words of praise. *Here

it comes*, I thought. *Ok, keep my eye on the ball, keep my eye on the

ball.* The ball was growing bigger by the millisecond. I kept *both* eyes on it. My glove was open, waiting, it was a good glove, Daddy bought it for me. SMACK! The ball was in my glove! I almost dropped it. I had to juggle it a little but it stayed in my glove.

"Good catch Chuckie!" I was brimming with pride as I looked up to see the grin on my dad's face. He wasn't there.

I heard the car backing out of the driveway and I ran around to the front of the house, to the street, just as the car started forward. I was suddenly very afraid and I jumped in front of it. My dad hit the brakes.

"You can't go!" I shouted, looking at him through the windshield. He got out, walked around to the front of the car, picked me up, and sat me on the hood.

"Chuckie, you know I have to go." He said. "We've been through this before. Do you remember?"

"Pick me up." I said, tears welling up in my eyes. He did and I hugged him tightly around the neck with all the strength my six-year–old arms could muster. He smelled great. It was his own unique scent. I can't describe it even now. It was just the way my dad smelled. I associated that smell with safety and strength, and I loved it.

"Chuckie, look at me." My dad said gently as he tried to pull back slightly so that he could see my face.

"No." I said. I buried my face in his neck, in his smell.

"Look at me son." He repeated softly. Reluctantly I loosened my grip and tilted my head back so that I could see his face.

"If I don't let you go," I said. "you'll stay with us." Only somehow I knew it wasn't true.

"No son, I still have to go, but this time I know what to say to you. Last time I wasn't really sure, and I was kind of afraid."

"You Daddy? You were afraid?" This was something I had simply never considered.

"Yes I was." He said as he brushed a tear from my cheek. "But I know now that I didn't need to be. There is nothing to be afraid of. That's what I want *you* to know."

"But there *is* Daddy." I cried. I'm afraid of *everything* without you here!"

"I'll always *be* here as long as you remember me." He said, smiling. I felt panicky and the tears were coming so fast now I felt sure we would be washed down the street in the flood of them.

"But Daddy, sometimes it's already hard to see your face. I'm afraid I'll forget. They might *make* me forget!"

"You won't forget." He said. "No matter what 'they' say or do, you and Brenda will help each other remember, and then someday we'll all be together again. *That's* the biggest thing you have to remember son. Can you do that for me?" He lowered me to the ground and knelt there in front of me. He hugged me to his chest and then led me off to the side of the road where he bent down and kissed me on the forehead.

"We'll all be together again. Remember that son." He backed away and headed around the front of the car to the driver's side. He climbed in and shut the door. Both windows were down and I looked through the passenger side at my dad, my hero.

"I'll remember Daddy." I whispered. He seemed to hear me and smiled warmly as the car began to pull away.

"Daddy!" I cried. "Can I tell anybody? Can I tell Brenda?"

The car never stopped, but I could hear his voice clearly, as if he was still with me, and I could feel it, as if it were some wondrous music . . . "You have to." He said. "You have to and you will."

When I awoke in the I.C.U at Goshen Hospital, no longer a six year old little boy, but once again a fifty-two year old walrus, I realized I had been crying for real. My pillow was soaked. I looked around, embarrassed, hoping no one had noticed. Apparently my secret was safe. I flipped the pillow over.

COMING BACK TO SHARE

I was very thankful this time around when I was told that I was being moved to Two North for my recovery period. I was wasted. The therapy dictates that you receive interleukin-2 until your body can't take any more. Well I do believe that my IL-2 cup was very close to runnething over after that sixth and final dose of the fifth cycle (and the moon was in the seventh house, and Jupiter aligned with Mars). I was told the therapy would kick my butt, and kicked, my butt thoroughly was.

As I lay there in my room on Two North, I felt as if I was almost in another dimension. I could see and hear what was going on around me and I could even respond just fine, but I seemed to be just kind of floating in and out of the room. I don't know where I floated out to because I was only conscious of the return float.

On one of these "outfloats" I attempted to remain cognizant. I recall losing the battle to keep my eyelids up, but then realizing that it didn't matter because I apparently could see through them. The first thing I noticed was that I wasn't floating at all.

I was walking, strolling if you will. My hands were in my pockets and they weren't the pockets of a pair of jeans that I had dreamed up from the past. They were in the pockets of the blue scrub pants I was wearing in real life. Lynn, one of the nurses on I.C.U. was nice enough to find me a set of scrubs that I could use for pajamas while I was recuperating on Two North. I had a pair of those gray, hospital footy things on my feet, and I was practically gliding down one of the shiny hospital corridors. I didn't know where I was headed but it felt good to be free of the puppet strings once again.

Suddenly I noticed a glow coming from around a set of double doors on my right. It didn't seem to be an ominous discovery. In fact I actually felt *eager* to pass through them, and I did.

I knew at once that I had just entered the hospital morgue. I had never actually seen Goshen Hospital's morgue before so I guess it looked like I expected it to look from TV. There were stainless steel tables and drawers in the walls where the bodies must be kept. It didn't creep me out as I would have expected. In fact I felt very comfortable there. I knew it must be chilly in the room, but the temperature felt just right to me.

The light I had seen coming from around the double door when I was outside, was coming from a smaller door that was set in the wall on the far side of the room. It was open only the slightest of cracks, but the light was so brilliantly white everything in the room was aglow with its intensity. This door didn't physically resemble the one I had seen while in the I.C.U. that time, but I understood them to be one and the same. I walked halfway across the room toward the door and then stopped. Did I want to go through? Yes, I realized, I did. Should I? I knew it would be all right if I did, *everything* would be all right. And not just all right, *wondrous*! I was very welcome, I could feel it, but I still was not *compelled* to go through. Suddenly I was back in my room on Two North and there was a nurse speaking to me.

"Mr. Walton, you need to wake up." She said. There was concern in her voice. I smiled up at her but now I can't remember which one she was. I felt very weak. "Your heart rate dropped to thirty Mr. Walton. Can you wake up for me? I need you to stay awake for a while." I think I responded, but I don't remember what I said. I stayed awake though.

I stayed awake because I began to remember my dream. I realized that approaching "the door" corresponded to the severe drop in my heart rate and it sort of gave me the old heebie-jeebies. As a matter of fact, by the next night I was extremely tired and desperately needed to sleep but I was afraid to. In my conscious - but fuzzy - state of mind I was afraid that I would fall asleep and go strolling through that door whether I was supposed to or not. I mean, in the dream it seemed that I was on the fence, that I could go either way, and neither way was the *wrong* way. Just the thought of being on the "threshold" of such a decision scared me awake.

I know that I've told you that I have come to grips with the whole dying thing, and I have. I no longer have any doubt whatsoever that we move on after this life. I don't just *believe* it now either, I *know* it. It's just that in my physical consciousness I still had trouble getting past the notion that I would miss those that I love unbearably.

I remembered the words of my daughter Autumn when I told her that I was ok with dying. She said, crying, "Well that's just fine Dad if *you're* ok with it, but *I'm not!* I need to know you're there in my life. Who's going to give me away at my wedding?" I guess I hadn't considered the fact that others would miss me as much as I would miss them. In fact, in the next life it is entirely possible that we are not capable of a negative feeling such as sadness, but the people we leave behind still are.

That's one of the reasons that I now believe it to be very important that we share with those we love, the fact that we will indeed all be together again when it's time for them to join us. (The other reason? My Dad told me to.)

That means that the burden to lessen the grief of loss and the feelings of despair felt by loved ones, falls to the person who is at risk of dying, not the other way around.

Not having thought all this through yet, or realizing the importance of my dreams, I couldn't get the thought of my ticker dropping down to thirty beats off my mind. Consequently, I couldn't, or wouldn't, sleep. At about 3:am of the morning following that last dream - more than twenty-four hours after, with no sleep - my nurse Rhoda came in to check on me and I confided in her my fear of falling asleep and not waking up. Rhoda could have simply said everything would be all right and then gone about her business, dismissing what I had said as the irrational fear of a silly old walrus. But she didn't. She sat down and began to tell me all the medical and technical reasons that I shouldn't have to worry about my heart stopping while I was sleeping. She told me that she was monitoring me all the time so I was never really alone. She stayed there with me until a lot of my confidence had returned. I found that what she had explained to me made so much sense that I decided I was worrying disproportionately and I told myself to knock it off. I knew at that point that when I had returned from that last dream, I had come back – at least for now - to stay.

And then I slept, this time dreamlessly.

MY NEW "FRIEND" LYMPHEDEMA

I mentioned my lymphedema before - the condition brought on by the fact that I no longer have any lymph nodes in my left leg. I was scared into taking it seriously by the elephant-leg photo, remember? Well, that's not the only reason I take it seriously anymore because now I know it can hurt like a son-of-a-gun! It sometimes starts aching and stinging from the inside out as if the fluid (also known as lymph) wants to just bust right through my skin. It actually feels like my skin will split open sometimes, but it hasn't yet.

Are you thinking you wish I'd quit whining? Ok, I'm finished.

I hadn't been to see Dr. Klauer at the lymphedema clinic in South Bend since that first time when he told me to make sure I had those "heat blisters" checked out. The lymphedema had become secondary to the IL-2 therapy, but now that that was behind me, Dr. Schwartzentruber suggested that I follow through. I could have gotten the lymphedema therapy at Goshen Hospital too, but since I had already been approved by Medicaid to see Dr. Klauer, and he had been the one who first expressed a concern about the new nodules, and he was closer to home, I returned there.

Dr. Klauer remembered me and we had quite a talk about my experience with the IL-2 therapy and the issues it had brought forth in my life. I was very surprised when Dr. Klauer looked me in the eye and said, "So where is God in all this for you?" I mean, how often do you hear a question like that from a physician? It was refreshing to say the least. I began looking forward to my visits to his clinic and thought to myself how well Dr. Klauer and the people on his staff would fit in with the great people over in Goshen.

They seem to follow the same "mind, body, *and* spirit" philosophy.

My lymphedema therapy went well. Amy was my therapist and she was great. The therapy involves redirecting the lymph in my leg through light massage followed up every day with compression bandages wrapped in a specific pattern. The idea is for the fluid to find new paths, side streets and back alleys, as they say, because it couldn't drain the way it was designed to anymore. Eventually my leg was a reasonable size again and it was time for me to begin maintaining it on my own.

Amy took leg measurements and ordered my compression stocking. When it arrived she showed me how to put it on with the least amount of difficulty - geez that thing is tight! I will be wearing this stocking during the daytime for the rest of my life. At night I am supposed to continue to wrap my leg with the compression bandages so Amy taught me the proper procedure for that.

With the expert help of Dr. Klauer, Amy, and Jane I feel confident that we can keep this lymphedema thing under the elephant-leg size I still have nightmares about from that photo.

THAT'S MY STORY AND I'M STICKIN TO IT

It is now November 2006. It has been over two years since I

was first diagnosed with melanoma, and almost a year since my last IL-2 therapy. As we know, metastatic melanoma is, c'mon, say it with me now, ALMOST always fatal. And I can still say that, even though there has recently been a small glitch here.

Just before this book was to go to press, I had my usual blood work and PET scan. This was the first time that my scans had been six months apart (Immediately after the IL-2 therapy they had been one month apart and then had gone to three.). This time Dr. Schwartzentruber saw four or five "hot spots" when he read the results. Yes, this means the melanoma has shown up again. It is a persistent son-of-a-gun, isn't it? It hangs on like a . . . oh, I don't know . . .like a cancer. It also means that I have to revise this text and correct a couple of statistics. I am not in the six per cent that have seen their melanoma totally eradicated by the IL-2. But I *am* in the thirteen percent who benefit from having a heck of a lot of it wiped out. No kidding. Without it, and everything else I speak of within these pages, there is no doubt in my mind that the cancer would have spread to my vital organs long ago and I would not be writing *anything* right now, let alone this book. The "hot spots" that have just been found, are in lymph nodes just above my left leg, (making the melanoma officially "stage four") but will be surgically removed, so I am leaving my title intact: *<u>Almost</u> Always Fatal.* None of that negative energy here!

Remember, one is a survivor "from the moment they are diagnosed with the cancer". Thinking positively, if I am alive two years from now, will I say to people that I have been dying from cancer for four years? Ridiculous! I will have been *surviving* cancer for four years.

The fact that I can still use the word "almost" in my title is my proof, dear reader, that I was supposed to write this book (and perhaps many more) for you. The fact that you are reading it, is *your* proof that you are seeking the positive, and that you are on the right track.

Besides entertaining you, which I most sincerely hope my story did, it was also supposed to scream out from the rooftops the following:

Take skin cancer seriously! It's no joke and can be deadly. Don't ignore things that suddenly appear, or change, or appear to change. Never let yourself get badly sunburned. Hey, I was the type that didn't burn easily too. But a couple of times, way back when I was about sixteen, I was at the beach at Lake Michigan all day long with no sunscreen of any kind (Shoot, sun screen back then didn't really exist. Baby oil seemed to be the big thing then.) and I was badly burned both times. The consensus of opinion is that that is probably when the melanoma got its start.

Proleukin is out there! You don't have to find out about it by chance like I did. It's the genetically engineered form of interleukin-2. The last I heard, IL-2 therapy was being done in seventeen locations throughout the country and of course I highly recommend the Center For Cancer Care in Goshen, Indiana. Does my recommendation mean anything? Of course it does, I'm around to write this book - longer than I might have been in years gone by!

Believe you have a soul! Don't worry; I'm not going to get all goofy on you here. But *I* know you have one. If *you* don't, a fat lot of good it'll do you. There is great healing power to be found in the goodness within you, in your essence, your direct link with infinite wisdom, which of course is God.

Seek a second opinion! And a third! If ever a doctor tells you that you have a serious condition, sickness, or ailment, take it seriously. Research it on the web. Find out as much as you can about it so you will know which questions to ask and where there might be new therapies that could benefit you. I'll say it again: *I found Dr. Schwartzentruber and the interleukin-2 therapy completely by accident.* If you recall, the other doctor, the "melanoma specialist", went on vacation and I was panicky and needed answers which put the local oncologist on the spot and forced him to call around until somebody finally said, "Well duh, there *is* that Dr. Schwartzentruber guy over there in Goshen." That's not an actual quote obviously, but the point is: The cancer doctors in my area all knew of Dr. Schwartzentruber and The Center for Cancer Care in Goshen, Indiana, but seemed to be reluctant to offer up this information. Remember, *they were going to strip all the rest of the skin off my leg when it wasn't necessary!* There is a very good chance that I would not have lived to write these words because of infection "complications".

I'd better settle down. I'm getting a little hot under the collar here.

Immerse yourself in positive energy! Negative thoughts on your part, and negative comments from others can only do you harm. Keep close around you those who consistently offer you hope, those who look you in the eye with a smile upon their lips because they sincerely care and are extending their love. People who can't look at you because they feel guilty that you are afflicted and they are not, are full of negative energy and you need to stay away from them.

Our leaving this life is <u>not</u> the responsibility of others! If even the *possibility* exists that one will soon be moving on from the physical realm to the spiritual, I believe from what I have personally experienced that the person doing the "moving on" is meant to bear the weight of reassuring those who will be left behind. The loved ones whom we are temporarily leaving should be comforted with the knowledge that there is happiness ahead, and joyous reunion!

Whenever the time arrives that you too are close to "the door", you will have no doubt that these words are true. I'm telling you now because your loved ones need to hear this assurance from you. They need the security of this truth to hang on to until the day arrives when it becomes their message to pass on in turn.

Take massive doses of the medication we call laughter! There is absolutely nothing better than humor for chasing away negative thoughts, feelings, and influences. Keep your spirit light. As you have seen from my own story this isn't always an easy thing to do. That's because we are constantly battling fears that are as old as man.

The fear of loss, of losing all contact with our loved ones, is really the fear of loneliness, for none of us can bear the thought of being totally alone in this vast universe. That is a mortal fear conceived of a mortal mindset.

Physically, we are so limited in our ability to transcend both space and time that it is entirely feasible to us that we could be isolated from those we love. Once you learn to meditate and get through all the garbage that you have collected throughout your life so that you can experience, even in this small way, the level of your own soul, you will know that who you really are, your spiritual self, knows no boundaries or restrictions. You cannot be kept from the love of those you cherish.

You are, in fact, composed of that love.

The fear of the unknown is the other biggie of the mortal mindset. In our purest form, our souls, our source of positive energy, the energy of goodness, of God, there is nothing that is unknown. That kind of nicely takes care of that one doesn't it?

My point is: If you can understand these things to be true, you have great cause for merriment. You can find the humor in things that might not have seemed all that funny before.

You will know that you are filled with the positive when someone says to you, "Geez, I can't believe you can find anything funny in this. If I were in *your* shoes, I would be so down and depressed that they might as well just scribble 'THE END' across my forehead!"

And you can say to them, "But I would never let that happen to *you* my friend. I would make them print it *neatly*."

BELIEVE

Printed in the United States
91612LV00007B/211-228/A